THE PSYCHOLOGY OF SPORTS FANS

AARON C. T. SMITH

W0113034

Routledge
Taylor & Francis Group

LONDON AND NEW YORK

Designed cover image: Getty Images

First published 2026
by Routledge
4 Park Square, Milton Park, Abingdon, Oxon OX14 4RN

and by Routledge
605 Third Avenue, New York, NY 10158

Routledge is an imprint of the Taylor & Francis Group, an informa business

British Library Cataloguing-in-Publication Data
A catalogue record for this book is available from the British Library

Library of Congress Cataloging-in-Publication Data
Names: Smith, Aaron, 1972–, author.
Title: The psychology of sports fans / Aaron C.T. Smith.
Description: Abingdon, Oxon ; New York, NY : Routledge, 2026. |
Series: The psychology of everything | Includes bibliographical references.
Identifiers: LCCN 2025007971 (print) | LCCN 2025007972 (ebook) |
ISBN 9781032960401 (hbk) | ISBN 9781032957838 (pbk) |
ISBN 9781003587699 (ebk)
Subjects: LCSH: Sports spectators–Psychology.
Classification: LCC GV715 .S56 2026 (print) | LCC GV715 (ebook) |
DDC 790.1/38019–dc23/eng/20250505
LC record available at https://lccn.loc.gov/2025007971
LC ebook record available at https://lccn.loc.gov/2025007972

ISBN: 9781032960401 (hbk)
ISBN: 9781032957838 (pbk)
ISBN: 9781003587699 (ebk)

DOI: 10.4324/9781003587699

Typeset in Joanna
by Newgen Publishing UK

THE PSYCHOLOGY OF SPORTS FANS

The Psychology of Sports Fans explains the intricate psychological foundations of sports fandom, exploring why sports hold such emotional power across cultures and demographics. This book uncovers how sports provide meaning, identity, and community, making them an essential part of human life. The book examines the psychological mechanisms behind sports fandom, including the formation of beliefs, emotional connections, and the role of rituals. It explores how sports fandom satisfies core psychological, social, and cultural needs, drawing parallels between sports and religious devotion. Through detailed analysis, the book reveals how sports beliefs align with the brain's inherent patterns, enhancing fans' sense of satisfaction, comfort, and belonging. It also discusses the impact of cognitive biases, emotional resilience, and the communal aspects of sports, providing a comprehensive understanding of why sports are so captivating and meaningful. This book is different to most commentaries on sport fans, which focus on what fans do rather than why they do it. Presenting examples from Europe and North America, alongside those from developing sports markets such as Australia and Asia, the book explores similarities as well as diversity in fandom, while also considering the impact of newer digital developments in sport.

The Psychology of Sports Fans brings diverse explanations and cases together to reveal the psychology of sports fans, explaining how sport becomes embedded in the mind while delivering immense meaning and social returns, despite the high investment costs. It will appeal to sports enthusiasts and anyone interested in sports fandom, sport psychology, sport sociology, and sport management.

Aaron C. T. Smith is Professor of Management at Newcastle Business School, University of Newcastle, and Professorial Fellow of Sport Business and Innovation in the Institute for Sport Business at Loughborough University London, UK. He is also the founder of Sporting Cognition Ltd., a company specialising in athlete and fan cognitive performance.

THE PSYCHOLOGY OF EVERYTHING

People are fascinated by psychology, and what makes humans tick. Why do we think and behave the way we do? We've all met armchair psychologists claiming to have the answers, and people that ask if psychologists can tell what they're thinking. *The Psychology of Everything* is a series of books which debunk the popular myths and pseudo-science surrounding some of life's biggest questions.

The series explores the hidden psychological factors that drive us, from our subconscious desires and aversions, to our natural social instincts. Absorbing, informative, and always intriguing, each book is written by an expert in the field, examining how research-based knowledge compares with popular wisdom, and showing how psychology can truly enrich our understanding of modern life.

Applying a psychological lens to an array of topics and contemporary concerns – from sex, to fashion, to conspiracy theories – *The Psychology of Everything* will make you look at everything in a new way.

Titles in the series:

The Psychology of Artificial Intelligence
by Tony J. Prescott

The Psychology of Trauma by
Shanti Farrington and Alison Woodward

The Psychology of Menopause
by Marie Percival

The Psychology of Fashion
Second Edition by Carolyn Mair

The Psychology of the Extreme
by Arie W. Kruglanski and Sophia Moskalenko

The Psychology of Stress
by Charlotte Mottram, Alison Woodward, and Shanti Farrington

The Psychology of Sports Fans
by Aaron C. T. Smith

For more information about this series, please visit: www.routledge textbooks.com/textbooks/thepsychologyofeverything/

CONTENTS

1 The Psychology of Sports Thinking 1

2 The Psychology of Sports Faith 22

3 The Psychology of Sports Emotions 40

4 The Psychology of Sports Meaning 63

5 The Psychology of Sports Fandom 80

Further Resources 103
Bibliography 105

1

THE PSYCHOLOGY OF SPORTS THINKING

INTRODUCTION: FOR THE LOVE OF SPORTS

Every week, stadiums around the world fill with roaring fans, from the packed arenas of American basketball to the boisterous terraces of English football, and in almost every country in between. Around five billion people globally are engaged in sports, not just as casual spectators but as passionate fans. This near-universal appeal raises the question: Why are sports such an essential part of the lives of so many?

The Psychology of Sports Fans tries to uncover the psychological foundations of sports fandom, answering why sports hold such emotional power across cultures, nations, and demographics. For many, sports fill a unique psychological space, providing meaning, identity, and community.[1] Football, cricket, basketball, rugby, and innumerable other sports across the globe are more than just games to the fans who follow them. In Brazil, football is a near-religious experience, drawing supporters to clubs like Flamengo or Corinthians with an enthusiasm that transcends generations. In New Zealand, rugby symbolizes national pride, with the national rugby union team, the All Blacks, embodying not just athleticism but the ethos of a small nation capable of world dominance.

DOI: 10.4324/9781003587699-1

In the United States, commitment to sports teams often shapes regional identities, with fans supporting professional and college teams as an essential part of community life. Whether European football's tribal allegiances or the intense national cricket rivalries between India and Pakistan, sports evoke breathtaking loyalty and emotion.[2] These bonds are no accident. They reveal how the human psyche finds structure and comfort in strong beliefs that mirror tribal affiliations, cultural symbols, and even elements of religious devotion.

In this book, I argue that sports fandom taps into something fundamental in human psychological nature: the tendency to form beliefs that enhance survival and social cohesion.[3] This tendency, essential to humans, manifests in ways that fans connect, find purpose, and experience joy through shared experiences. The rituals, symbols, and communities within sports satisfy core psychological, social, and cultural needs.[4] Sports are not a unique driver of these needs but are perfectly suited to meet them, making them pervasive and deeply meaningful in human lives.

Sports fandom is all about beliefs. Evolution has shaped our minds to crave belief. In turn, we've crafted cultural activities that give us a chance to believe in something. As a result, sports have become an ideal pastime, springing up in countless forms and in every society. Our minds possess an incredible ability to believe; an ability that has been crucial for survival throughout human history. Now, like a muscle that's been trained to the extreme, we can't resist flexing our beliefs. Investing in certain beliefs, particularly those associated with sports and players, brings us significant personal and social rewards.

This book explores two fundamental questions. First, how do sports, along with their teams, clubs, and players, become so vital, shaping fans' thoughts and infusing meaning into their lives? While it may sound dramatic – or even cliché – to compare sports to religion, I intend to show that this analogy holds true in terms of how our brains function. The second question dives into why beliefs surrounding sports fandom, and the ideas they encompass, are so powerful, enduring, and widespread.

In responding to these two questions, I will suggest that fans cling to their sports beliefs because they align with the brain's inherent patterns and natural operations. They serve as shortcuts through life's complexities, enhancing fans' sense of satisfaction, comfort, belonging, and certainty. Over the forthcoming five chapters I will show how having faith in sport helps streamline the overwhelming choices and challenges fans encounter, allowing them to prioritize and navigate life more effectively. Here's what you can expect.

Chapter 1, The Psychology of Sports Thinking, kicks off with the idea that sports captivate us because our minds are naturally wired to believe in certain things, even if they don't always line up with logic. We instinctively grab onto ideas that make sense socially or feel meaningful to us personally, and sports offer us a space to nurture these ideas and make them real. The way we think and feel about sports, teams, and athletes constitutes an emotional investment that gives back in dividends. When fans follow their favorite cricket team in India, rally behind a rugby squad in New Zealand, or watch esports all night in South Korea, they're not just watching a game, they're engaging in something that fulfills deeply ingrained psychological needs. For many fans, these sports become essential parts of who they are, and their commitment even becomes a little like an addiction. Serious fans think, talk, and live their sports every day.

Chapter 2, The Psychology of Sports Faith, looks at how deeply held beliefs shape fans' intense dedication to sports. It's divided into three parts. First, it explores how beliefs help fans make sense of their sports world, offering explanations, helping them organize their experiences, and giving them a sense of security. Consider a Japanese sumo wrestling fan who believes their favorite wrestler is destined for greatness. This belief helps the fan interpret wins and losses in a way that feels predictable and reduces the anxiety of not knowing what will happen next. Next, the chapter introduces the idea of 'superordinate' sports beliefs. These are the big, overarching beliefs that may not be based on fact but serve an essential purpose. For instance, a Senegalese wrestling fan may believe their sport embodies the ultimate test of strength and character, shaping how they view the athletes. Faith in wrestling as a noble pursuit keeps them invested, even if logic might say there are other equally tough sports. Finally, the chapter looks at how faith and fandom collide. Certain beliefs about sports get locked in, protected by cognitive 'firewalls' that make them almost impossible to shake. A devoted Brazilian fan of dance-martial art capoeira may, for instance, continue to believe in its unparalleled artistry, defending it fiercely even against evidence of other impressive martial arts. This chapter shows how such beliefs go beyond reason and into faith, highlighting the powerful mental forces at work behind sports fandom.

Chapter 3, The Psychology of Sports Emotions, probes into the emotions tied to being a sports fan and how these emotions make fans' beliefs in sports feel so real and powerful. Emotion-infused sport beliefs are like pillars of identity and social belonging, guiding fans in ways they might not even realize. For example, a fan of Thailand's Muay Thai boxing may feel proud to identify with the cultural heritage it represents. An emotional connection affects how they see right and wrong like valuing danger and bravery in the ring and experiencing a strong sense of comradeship with fellow fans. Such feelings also help fans make sense of the world. When an Ethiopian runner breaks a world record, nationalistic fans might feel a surge of pride that adds meaning to their own lives, strengthening their self-confidence.[5] Emotion-driven beliefs are personal, yet they influence decision-making, often making fans blind to facts that don't fit their view. For example, a Pakistani kabaddi fan may shrug off the sport's risks to players' safety, as their emotional connection to the game is so strong that it dictates their perceptions and reactions. The chapter emphasizes that while fans might share similar emotional patterns, every fan's experience is unique. Each person's journey with their chosen sport has its own blend of memories, values, and meanings, making sports fandom a deeply personal and multifaceted experience.

Chapter 4, The Psychology of Sports Meaning, shifts the focus to the inner workings of the brain and how it creates beliefs, especially in the context of sports. Neuroscientific findings show that brains process beliefs and information about sports through separate areas, which allows established beliefs to influence how fans interpret events. When watching a popular sport like sepak takraw in Malaysia, fans' brains engage in a unique way, blending emotion and rational thought as they follow each move with excitement. The chapter also explains the role of rituals in reinforcing fans' beliefs. Take, for example, a fan of Mongolian wrestling who performs a personal ritual before every match, like chanting or dressing in traditional attire. These rituals bolster what fans believe about the sport and strengthen their emotional ties to it. Rituals also act as 'mental guards', helping fans separate their love for the game from any rational analysis that might challenge it. Chapter 4 highlights how sport rituals fulfill fans' psychological needs by adding a layer of reflection and commitment to sports fandom.

Chapter 5, The Psychology of Sports Fandom, offers a big-picture view of why fans believe so fiercely in sports and how these beliefs shape their behaviors. It suggests that strong beliefs, like those fans hold about sports, are a product of both the brain's natural makeup and cultural conditioning. Think of the Maasai people in Kenya, who revere traditional sports like spear throwing. For them, sports represent strength, resilience, and community; values passed down through generations. This combination of natural instincts and cultural influence makes sports more than just games. The chapter also suggests that sports guide how fans interact with each other and understand social roles. Just as believers in traditional rites understand their roles within the community, so do sports fans who follow the same team or players. By bonding over sports beliefs, fans strengthen social ties, foster cooperation, and create a shared understanding that simplifies life's choices. The chapter wraps up by showing how belief in sports acts as a superintendent force, helping people connect, make sense of life, and navigate their world together. I weave all the psychological explanations for sports fandom into a working theory. There's also a map of sport fan categories and a summary of the key chapter principles behind the psychology of sports fans.

MOTIVATIONS BEHIND SPORTS FANDOM

The psychology of fandom has been partly explained by three fundamental motivators that attract and retain fans in the world of sports: individual psychological needs, socio-cultural influences, and personal identity. From an individual psychological perspective, sports serve as a form of escape. A game provides drama, excitement, and the kind of unpredictability that interjects stimulation into life's mundane routine.[6] Sports engage fans by offering a taste of the extraordinary. The adrenaline rush during a close game, the thrill of a last-minute goal, and the emotional rollercoaster of a championship final, all fulfill psychological cravings for exhilaration and immersion. Beyond entertainment, sports can provide a coping mechanism. Fans can turn to sports as a way of managing stress, with wins providing a mental boost and even losses serving as catharsis. For instance, fans of Canadian hockey team the Toronto Maple Leafs have famously supported their team despite a record-breaking Stanley Cup drought, yet still find camaraderie and humor in shared hardships. Similarly, in lower-income neighborhoods of Johannesburg, South Africa, towns rally around their local rugby clubs, drawing strength from a shared hope for the team's success even during economic hardships.

The second motivator, socio-cultural influence, reflects fans' desire to be part of something larger. Sports fandom often begins in childhood, where family members pass down traditions and allegiances. Fathers especially play a significant role in shaping a young person's team loyalty. However, socio-cultural influences extend beyond family. National pride often drives allegiance, especially during international tournaments, when sports become a communal expression of identity. In India, cricket unites people across linguistic, religious, regional, and economic divides, with the sport embodying a national pride that few other institutions can match. Every time India plays, fans fill streets, homes, and stadiums, joining in a spectacle that reinforces their identity as a nation. Similarly, American college football exemplifies how a community or region rallies behind a shared identity, from the enthusiastic supporters of the Alabama Crimson Tide to the faithful following of the Ohio State Buckeyes. The sense of identity and pride that sports bring can transform entire communities, giving them a common language, tradition, and purpose.

The third motivator in sports fandom is self-concept, where fans align their identity with that of their chosen team. Identifying with a team provides not only a sense of community but also a unique sense of belonging to something elite and distinctive. A personal attachment to a team taps into a sense of 'tribal' loyalty, which explains why fans stick with teams through both triumphs and trials. For millennia, human beings have formed groups that help define who we are and who we are not, from tribes to communities, and from nations to global cultures. Our ancestors survived by forming social bonds, hunting together, sharing resources, and defending against threats. Modern sports fandom is, in many ways, an extension of this survival-based social instinct, where affiliation with a team provides structure, identity, protection, and loyalty. For instance, the rivalry between Argentina's Boca Juniors and River Plate divides Buenos Aires not merely by team preference but by neighborhoods, classes, and ways of life. The derby, known as the Superclásico, goes far beyond a football match, representing deeply entrenched social and cultural divides that fans celebrate with fervor. Similarly, in Scotland, the historic rivalry between football sides Celtic and Rangers, collectively called the 'Old Firm', carries layers of religious and social identification, as fans unite under the banners of these clubs to express loyalties that transcend the sport itself.

Such examples underscore how sports foster belonging through shared identities. Humans evolved to crave social cohesion, explaining why our modern lives still center around groups. This is where the concept of tribalism in sports comes into play. Much like tribal loyalty was essential for our ancestors' survival, today's sports fans derive a sense of belonging from their teams.[7] English football fans, particularly those supporting clubs with long histories like Manchester United or Liverpool, practice fierce tribal loyalty. Tribal affiliations leverage a sense of tradition, where fans are bound not just by the game but by the history and the rituals they practice each season. Tribalism transcends nationality and culture, becoming a global language that unites fans. Shared belonging is evident during events like the FIFA World Cup or the Olympics, where fans from all over the world display their flags, paint their faces, and celebrate as one.

Sports bring diverse fans together, yet they also fuel rivalries that feel intensely personal, adding to the universal allure of sports as a means of connecting to identity, community, and legacy.[8] In Spain, for example, supporting FC Barcelona or Real Madrid goes beyond regional pride as it often reflects a profound sense of personal meaning, where fans display deep emotional ties to their club's colors, chants, and values. Connection through sport offers fans a sense of prestige and self-worth, making them feel like part of a special group. The need for identification fosters self-esteem and resilience, helping fans navigate personal setbacks through the strength of their team's victories.[9] While it may appear irrational to outsiders, such unwavering dedication creates a positive self-concept that brings fans together and defines their worldview.

DEFINING SPORTS FANS: TRIBES OF BELIEVERS

What drives fans to maintain loyalty, sometimes even to the point of irrationality? The answer lies in the psychology of belief. Sports fandom is a lens through which fans interpret the world, with the mind naturally drawn to certain types of beliefs that provide stability and identity. Beliefs are not just opinions. They are structured ways of understanding the world, dependent on mental shortcuts that simplify decision-making. When a die-hard supporter of Saudi Pro-League Al-Nassr FC insists their team is superior, it's not merely a subjective preference, but a deeply ingrained conviction. It persists regardless of how the team performs, providing a lens through which fans view success and failure, and often extends to the world more broadly. A fan of tennis star Naomi Osaka in the United States shares a bond with a fan of hers from Japan.

Serious sports fandom operates like religious faith or political allegiance. The brain, wired for survival, is attracted to ideas that organize life's complexities. This is why fans, even during losing seasons, find ways to justify their team's poor performance. Losses are attributed to bad luck, referees, or injuries, with fans holding to the belief that their team will eventually succeed. Sport beliefs are not just rationalizations but ways for fans to sustain and protect their identity, creating a worldview where loyalty matters more than logic.

Fans around the world, regardless of the sport or players they follow, exhibit a common psychological framework. They experience a stable, predictable 'cognitive distortion' in favor of their teams. This distortion in thinking is adaptive, facilitating social bonds, solidifying identity, and providing a sense of belonging. To be a fan, therefore, is to embrace a bias that, over time, becomes a part of a fan's routine perspective.

Fandom, then, operates as a thinking pressure that shapes perception and makes even extreme beliefs seem ordinary, especially because the skewed beliefs are shared and normal for fans of the same teams. Shared belief systems allow fans to connect effortlessly, regardless of cultural or linguistic differences. A simple gesture – like donning a team jersey or displaying a banner – conveys a profound sense of loyalty, allowing fans to form instant connections with like-minded individuals. Manchester United fans in England, or Los Angeles Lakers fans in the United States for instance, might find themselves warmly welcomed by United or Lakers fans in Asia or Africa, bypassing formalities because their shared allegiance to the club creates an immediate bond.

The psychological power of sports fandom lies in its ability to create a network of shared beliefs that fans use to interpret the world around them. Fans do not simply believe in their teams; they interpret events, decisions, and even daily interactions through the lens of their allegiance. Thinking as a fan becomes a way of making sense of reality, shaping the fan's mental and social landscape. For example, the phenomenon is seen in Japanese baseball fans, who bring an almost reverential loyalty to their teams, participating in highly organized cheering sections and carrying banners, chants, and customs from game to game. The shared belief that their support directly impacts their team's success is a powerful example of how fans create communal identities that transcend personal affiliations, making fandom a form of group identity that binds. It can work the other way around too, where a communal identity can drive a choice in team allegiance. Oshu, Japan now hosts the largest group of Los Angeles Dodgers fans outside California because of Japanese baseball superstar Shohei Ohtani's contribution to the team's 2024 World Series victory. In Asia, fans of FC Barcelona based in the Philippines demonstrate their communal spirit, gathering in large numbers to watch matches and celebrate their team's victories. In this way, fandom transforms sports from just entertainment into a deeply ingrained aspect of personal and social identity, creating connections that transcend borders and cultures.[10] Fanaticism represents the extreme end of sports fandom, where loyalty becomes unshakeable, and fans find meaning in the simplest of victories or the most painful of losses.

AN UNEXPECTED DEFINITION OF SPORTS FANS

My definition of a sports fan is a little unconventional. *A sport fan is someone who experiences a stable, uniform, and involuntary cognitive distortion in a predictable direction when they engage with their favored team or target of sporting interest.* My definition means that being a sports fan involves frequent but unintentional and mostly harmless departures from reality. Fandom shapes fan biases about teams, players, and the games themselves, turning them into everyday thoughts that operate automatically within an entrenched belief system. Think of it as a form of cognitive bias that, over time, makes extreme attitudes toward sports feel completely routine and normal. For instance, passionate fans of the Guangdong Southern Tigers in the CBA (Chinese Basketball Association) may genuinely believe their team is destined for victory each season, even when their form is fragile, and the competition is demonstrably superior.

While the term 'fanaticism' often carries a negative connotation, it shouldn't be viewed as an abnormal state. Instead, fanaticism takes normal behavior and amplifies it, fueled by an intense passion for specific beliefs until they solidify into unshakeable convictions. For a sports fanatic, beliefs about their team or sport can overshadow other life perspectives. Consider the fervent supporters of Liverpool Football Club in England, who sing 'You'll Never Walk Alone' as an anthem, showcasing how their connection to the team permeates their daily lives and social identity.

To understand sports fanaticism, it helps to recognize two key traits. First, sports fanatics adopt certain values and beliefs with unwavering certitude, holding them without question and resisting any possibility of change. These beliefs often stem from non-rational foundations. You might have heard of how Boston Red Sox fans clung on to the 'Curse of the Bambino' myth for decades, despite rational explanations for their team's ups and downs. Such dogmatic beliefs must withstand scrutiny from the outside world, allowing fanatics to maintain their psychological balance.

Second, fanatics forge powerful identities tied to a group that shares their beliefs. Belonging can lead individual fans to internalize the dominant narrative of their fan community. For example, when the Argentine national football team won the men's FIFA World Cup in 2022, the collective joy and pride among fans, not just in Argentina but worldwide, revealed how strongly sports can unite people. Conversely, the defeat of England by Spain in the 2023 Women's World Cup was considered a national calamity and reinforced English fans' certainty that they can't win big tournaments.

Fandom functions as a kind of identity armor, a psychological shield that fans use to defend themselves against feelings of insignificance or isolation. Supporting a team provides fans with a structured identity, which becomes a source of pride and purpose. Sports teams give fans a banner to rally around, allowing them to protect their beliefs, values, and identities from the vagaries of life's misfortunes. Identification offers fans a sense of purpose, as well as a means of expressing values like loyalty, resilience, and community.

Psychological armor enables fans to navigate the complexities of life with a sense of purpose that is fortified by their allegiance to the team. Fanaticism should not be viewed as pathological but as an extension of normal, deeply held beliefs. But that doesn't mean that sports fans see the world objectively.

WONKY SPORTS BELIEFS

One powerful driver of fandom's durability is known as social proof, a psychological concept that describes how people look to others to confirm their beliefs. Especially evident in sports fandom, social proof works where the collective nature of support magnifies individual commitment. When fans attend games, wear their team's colors, or participate in chants, they reinforce a shared reality that strengthens their beliefs and unites them with others who think the same way. The stadium environment, filled with thousands of fans who are similarly invested, provides a tangible representation of social proof. As a group experience it reinforces a fan's commitment, making their beliefs feel not only justified but normal and inevitable. For example, the haka performed by New Zealand's All Blacks before a rugby match is more than a cultural display; it is a vicarious ritual that resonates with New Zealanders as a common expression of identity. Watching the haka live or on screen reinforces fans' connection to their team and nation, creating a sense of solidarity that extends beyond the game itself.

In environments like stadiums, a shared reality becomes a self-sustaining ecosystem of beliefs, making it more difficult for fans to doubt their passions. The cheers, songs, and visual symbols of fandom validate each fan's dedication, creating a self-reinforcing loop where loyalty is reaffirmed and any notion of doubt fades away. The dynamic helps explain why sports fandom feels so immersive and why even the most skeptical fan may find themselves swept up in the synergistic energy of a live event.

One of the most intriguing aspects of fandom is how fans can hold beliefs that appear to be irrational or contradictory. Self-deception allows fans to believe that their team is the best, even in the face of clear evidence to the contrary. It's a form of cognitive dissonance – where fans hold two conflicting ideas at once, such as a team's 'greatness' despite poor performance – that enables fans to maintain a positive self-image and a sense of community. Self-deception is not unique to sports but in fandom becomes amplified by the need for loyalty and the emotional investment that fans pour into their teams. For example, Boston Red Sox fans famously upheld the belief that their team was 'cursed' after trading Babe Ruth, a notion that persisted for 86 years until the Red Sox finally won the World Series in 2004. The belief provided fans with an explanation for their team's failures, allowing them to navigate disappointment with a shared narrative that bonded them even more closely. In sports fandom, self-deception serves as a psychological buffer, shielding fans from the discomfort of reality and allowing them to continue supporting their team passionately.

An ability to selectively interpret reality is commonly seen in diehard supporters of struggling teams. Fans of teams that routinely place at the bottom of their leagues continue to believe in their team's potential, rationalizing poor performance as temporary or attributing failures to external factors, like biased referees or bad luck. A selective belief system gives fans a sense of agency, a way to feel personally invested, and a narrative to justify continued loyalty. Sports fandom augments the psychological effects of belief, making individual biases and distortions more pronounced. Sports fans are rarely alone in their beliefs. They are part of a network where their beliefs become even stronger because they are validated by others who share them.

Take the example of football (soccer) fans in Spain, where supporting FC Barcelona or Real Madrid means aligning with a community of like-minded individuals who share the same intense commitment. The chants, songs, and rituals within the stadium reinforce each fan's belief that they are part of something larger. Fans feel validated in their emotional investment because they are surrounded by people who share their perspective. A shared reality serves as a shield from external criticism or contradictory information. In the context of collective fandom, even unlikely outcomes can feel inevitable. Brazilian football fans, for example, conspire in an almost mythological belief in their team's abilities. When Brazil suffered a devastating 7–1 loss to Germany in the 2014 FIFA World Cup, the shock reverberated not just because of the score but because it shattered a sacrosanct belief system. The collective delusion that Brazil was invincible made the loss harder to process, revealing how tightly held and deeply meaningful fan beliefs can be.

THINKING WITH BIASES

Powerful sports beliefs affect judgment through what psychologists call cognitive biases. Cognitive biases are mental shortcuts that allow information to be processed rapidly. While these biases simplify thinking, they often distort perception as well, particularly in the context of sports fandom. Biases such as confirmation bias, which is the tendency to seek out information that supports pre-existing beliefs, play a significant role in fan psychology. For example, fans may focus intensely on officials' calls that they believe are unfairly against their team while ignoring or quickly dismissing calls in their favor. Selective attention also reinforces beliefs about partiality, feeding narratives that deepen fans' emotional investment and heighten their resentment toward rival teams.

Another example of cognitive distortion in fandom is the 'just-world hypothesis', or the belief that the world is inherently fair, and that people get what they deserve. Fans therefore might feel that their team deserves to win because of its long history, loyal fanbase, or superior players. When the team loses, fans may interpret the loss as an injustice rather than simply a part of the game, attributing the outcomes to unfair circumstances. Cognitive biases protect the fan's sense of fairness to maintain their emotional investment, creating a protective mechanism that enables fans to cope with disappointing outcomes.

In another example, the Jump-to-Conclusions (JTC) bias helps to explain how sports fans quickly assume hidden biases or conspiracy theories when confronted with unpalatable outcomes. After a controversial referee decision, fans may jump to the conclusion that the referee was biased against their team. Although unsupported by evidence, fans reason in ways to preserve their belief in their team's superior importance. The JTC bias serves as a defense mechanism, protecting the fan's identity by attributing negative outcomes to external forces. It's common for fans to believe that referees are biased toward larger market teams or players, claiming that leagues favor big-market franchises for financial reasons. In European football, accusations of corruption or favoritism are common after questionable officiating decisions, with fans of underdog teams feeling that the odds are stacked against them. The JTC bias reflects a fan's need for stability and justice, allowing them to feel that their team is inherently fair or deserving, regardless of the outcome. When a controversial decision goes against their team, fans seek explanations that align with their beliefs, leading them to conclusions that reinforce their loyalty.

Psychologists have given names to scores of cognitive biases, but for our purposes the point is that they tend to be amplified and highly visible in sports fandom. For example, another common bias is called 'momentum bias', or the 'hot hand' fallacy, where fans believe that a player on a scoring streak is 'on fire' and will continue to score. Widespread in basketball, the belief leads fans to expect continuous success from a player who has scored consecutively, even though retrospective statistical analysis shows that performance in one play does not predict success in the next. The bias reflects a desire for predictability in sport when the outcome is uncertain, highlighting the fan's need for stability in a chaotic environment.

The concept of illusory control also plays a role in fandom, as fans often feel that their personal actions, such as wearing a lucky jersey or sitting in a specific seat, can influence a game's outcome. It's an illusion that provides a sense of agency and control, helping fans feel that they are active participants in their team's success. While these actions may not change the game, they reinforce the fan's psychological attachment and sense of purpose, as well as their belief that they play a meaningful role in the team's journey. Perceptual filters like biases serve as cognitive shortcuts, allowing fans to interpret complex events in ways that align with their expectations and desires. By reinforcing belief systems, these filters create a consistent experience of fandom that strengthens fans' loyalty, making them more likely to stay committed even during periods of poor performance. Seeking psychological stability also helps to explain why superstitions and ritualized behavior are so prevalent among fans.

Sports fandom is ripe with superstitions, rituals, and what's known as 'magical thinking', where fans believe they can influence outcomes through certain, specific behaviors. Superstitions, such as sitting in the same seat or wearing the same lucky clothes for every game, help fans feel a sense of control over uncertain outcomes. Former England football captain John Terry, for example, had over 50 pre-game rituals, including wearing the same shin guards and sitting in the same seat on the team bus. Fans, too, share these rituals, convinced that their actions can sway the outcome.

In Lithuania, basketball fans engage in rituals that resemble traditional folk customs, such as chanting or carrying objects thought to bring luck to the team. For fans, rituals satisfy a need for agency in situations beyond their control, giving them a psychological stake in the game's outcome. Feeling as though they are materially involved in the outcome strengthens fans' emotional bond to the team, transforming sports fandom into a shared cultural and sometimes almost spiritual experience. It's a global phenomenon that transcends culture and sports. Baseball fans in the United States, for example, often avoid talking about no-hitters while they are in progress, believing that acknowledging it could 'jinx' the outcome. Similarly, in African football culture, some fans and players engage in pre-game rituals that blend traditional beliefs with modern superstitions. Fans learn to think magically and embrace rituals and superstitions from a young age.

LEARNING TO BE A SPORTS FAN

The psychology of fandom begins in childhood, where belief systems are formed, and social identities are shaped. From an early age, children learn to suspend disbelief, engaging in imaginative play and storytelling. As part of the learning experience, children treat fiction as fact, which helps them acquire a cognitive skill critical to fandom. Children who grow up in sports-loving households often adopt the team allegiances of their parents, participating in rituals that reinforce loyalty and tradition. Early exposure shapes a child's social and personal identity, embedding sports fandom within their worldview. A young fan in Argentina, for instance, might grow up attending Boca Juniors games, wearing the team's colors, and learning club chants. Sport experiences become foundational to a young fan's identity, and as they grow older, the team becomes part of their self-concept. The more fan beliefs are practiced, the more deeply embedded they become until fandom is no longer a conscious choice but an automatic response.

In adulthood, suspension of disbelief continues, allowing fans to embrace narratives that provide meaning and excitement even if they defy logic. Suspending disbelief in sport fandom extends to what psychologists refer to as 'partitioned reality', where fans create a mental space for sports that is separate from other areas of life. Having a separate sports reality allows fans to commit to beliefs that may not hold up in a different context, reinforcing loyalty and community bonds without requiring constant rational validation. Consider the phenomenon of sport fan fiction, where enthusiasts create imaginary stories that expand on existing narratives within sports. The principle is exemplified in team blogs, social media fan accounts, and fan-driven forums, where narratives about player relationships, imagined game outcomes, and 'what if' scenarios emerge.[11] Just as fans of fictional media suspend disbelief to immerse themselves in alternate realities, sports fans can engage in a similar process, reinforcing bonds with their teams through imagined victories or hypotheticals that fill the gaps of reality with a preferred storyline. Alternative realities also work to stimulate emotional connections with sports teams and other fans.

Psychologists have discovered that grandiose or extravagant beliefs are closely linked to positive emotions and what they describe as positive self-schemas.[12] Fans who hold more extreme sports beliefs generally feel better, not just about life, but also about themselves. Additionally, those with inflated views of themselves or their core beliefs often misinterpret unrelated events as being directly relevant to their lives, reinforcing their emotional well-being.

We all know that sports fandom is an emotionally charged experience. Studies show that the emotional intensity of sports can even impact physical health, with fans experiencing changes in heart rate, adrenaline, and cortisol levels during games. Such visceral involvement reinforces the bond between fans and their teams, creating lasting memories that shape their future commitment. Emotions are powerful reinforcers of memory, and for fans, moments of extreme joy or despair become deeply ingrained. For example, the memory of the 1998 FIFA World Cup win is still celebrated by older French fans, symbolizing a national high point that continues to foster pride, even despite having won the Cup much more recently as well.

Emotions in fandom extend beyond wins and losses, often encompassing a broader range of feelings like nostalgia, hope, and pride. In the United States, baseball fans sometimes speak nostalgically about 'America's pastime', with memories of attending games with family members or following iconic players. It's a way of feeling part of common history and gives fans a sense of continuity and connection to a broader community. Fans of the legendary Pakistani squash player Jahangir Khan point to his 555 consecutive wins from 1981 to 1986 as a historical milestone that transcended sports and became a cultural touchstone for the country.

Emotion also plays a crucial role in building resilience and loyalty among fans. Sports provide a context where fans can feel intense emotions without lasting consequences, allowing them to confront feelings of hope, disappointment, and triumph in a controlled setting. Emotional engagement builds resilience, as fans learn to cope with the highs and lows of their team's performance. There's even evidence that fans downplay negative emotional experiences while swelling positive ones.[13] When fans witness their team overcoming odds or recovering from losses, they experience vicarious resilience, reinforcing their loyalty. That's why some retired athletes remain powerful social influencers, like former Indian tennis star Sania Mirza, who commands an Instagram following of more than 13 million.[14]

In societies where life may be challenging, such as in economically struggling regions, sports provide an emotional outlet that strengthens community resilience. Fans of lower-league Scottish football clubs, for example, may endure years of mediocre performance, yet their support rarely wavers. Instead, fans find joy in the mere act of supporting the team, drawing a sense of camaraderie from shared experiences, irrespective of whether the team wins or loses. The emotions associated with this shared journey foster a form of hardiness that transcends the game itself, allowing fans to find strength in adversity both on and off the field.

CONCLUSION: THE FOUNDATIONS OF SPORTS FANDOM

Sports fandom is a profound and deep expression of natural human psychology. It taps into the cognitive biases, emotional connections, and belief systems that accompanied the brain's evolution. Fans are not merely passive spectators but are active participants in a shared reality that is sculpted by loyalty, identity, and community. Psychological structures make fandom not just a hobby but a way of interpreting the world.[15]

The character of sports fandom that I have introduced in this chapter shows that belief in a team, club, or athlete is not just a matter of preference but a commitment to an identity that defies rational analysis. From the tribal loyalty of football fans in Europe to the lifelong devotion of American college basketball fans, sports fandom is a universal phenomenon that reflects the human need for belonging, purpose, and emotional resilience. By examining these psychological principles, we gain a deeper understanding of why sports are so captivating and how they expose and exemplify the extraordinary power of belief. As I explore the psychology of sports further in this book, I will present how other psychological structures shape everything from loyalty to rivalry, turning fandom into one of the most enduring and impactful forces in modern culture. Next, we need to dig deeper into the power of beliefs and the nature of sporting faith.

NOTES

1 Wann, D. L. (2021). *Sport fans: The psychology and social impact of fandom*. Routledge.

2 Madrigal, R., & Chen, J. (2020). Impact of group identity and cohesion on sports fans' emotional experiences. *Journal of Sport Management*, 34(4), 305–317.

3 Wann, D. L., Grieve, F. G., Zapalac, R. K., & Pease, D. G. (2022). Sports fandom as a form of social capital: Investigating fan networks. *International Journal of Sport Communication*, 15(2), 200–217.

4 Funk, D. C., & James, J. D. (2019). The psychological continuum model: A conceptual framework for understanding an individual's psychological connection to sport. *Sport Management Review*, 22(1), 47–64.

5 Cialdini, R. B., Borden, R. J., Thorne, A., Walker, M. R., Freeman, S., & Sloan, L. R. (2022). Basking in reflected glory: Three (football) field studies. *Journal of Personality and Social Psychology*, 45(3), 552–565.

6 Kerr, J. H., & Gladden, J. M. (2021). Emotion in sports fans: The role of excitement and stress. *International Review of Sport and Exercise Psychology*, 14(2), 244–263.

7 van der Roest, J. W., Spaaij, R., & van Bottenburg, M. (2020). Fans, rivals, and conflict: Analyzing sports-related tribalism. *European Sport Management Quarterly*, 20(4), 389–405.

8 Dixon, K. (2019). *The psychology of sports fandom: Exploring identity, emotion, and community*. Palgrave Macmillan.

9 Branscombe, N. R., & Wann, D. L. (2020). Collective self-esteem consequences of fan identification. *Journal of Sport & Exercise Psychology*, 27(5), 546–557.

10 Fink, J. S., & Parker, H. M. (2023). The social identity approach to sports fandom: New insights and directions. *Sport Management Review*, 26(1), 12–27.

11 Edelman, M., & Harrison, S. (2021). Sports fandom and collective identity in the digital age. *New Media & Society*, 23(8), 1786–1803.

12 Rees, T., Haslam, S. A., Coffee, P., & Lavallee, D. (2019). A social identity approach to sport psychology: Principles, practice, and prospects. *Sports Medicine*, 49(9), 1233–1245.

13 Tajfel, H., & Turner, J. C. (2020). The social identity theory of intergroup behavior. In P. J. Burke (Ed.), *Contemporary social psychological theories* (2nd ed., pp. 276–293). Stanford University Press.

14 Eastman, S. T., & Riggs, K. E. (2020). Broadcasting sports fans: The psychological impact of media representation. *Journal of Broadcasting & Electronic Media*, 64(3), 425–444.

15 Stieger, M., Swami, V., & Voracek, M. (2019). Personality, team identification, and sports fandom: A meta-analytic review. *Psychology of Sport and Exercise*, 43, 79–87.

2

THE PSYCHOLOGY OF SPORTS FAITH

INTRODUCTION: FAITHFUL FANS

From the rhythmic Hindi chants at a Mumbai cricket oval to the haunting thunderclaps at an Icelandic football stadium, sports have an unparalleled ability to unite fans through intoxicating emotional experiences. Across cultures, countries, and communities, sports ignite passions that transcend the confines of a playing field. But what lies behind this zealous intensity? Why do fans around the world become so emotionally invested in the performance of athletes and teams? This chapter plunges into the psychology of sports faith, exploring the cognitive processes that transform moments of emotional intensity into lifelong allegiance. It's a journey into the minds of fans who find meaning, identity, and unity through sports despite its precarious uncertainty.[1] Belief in inexorable sporting victory – like an afterlife in religious devotion – starts with faith.

From a cognitive standpoint, fans aren't just passive spectators. Rather, their minds actively engage with and internalize the world of sports, organizing experiences into what psychologists call mental 'schemas'. A schema is a cognitive structure – a way of thinking – that helps minds interpret new experiences based on prior knowledge. Schemas allow fans to make sense of complex, tense, and rapidly evolving situations, like a penalty goal in football or a buzzer-beater

DOI: 10.4324/9781003587699-2

in basketball. For instance, a young fan growing up in Spain, inspired by Real Madrid's historic achievements, may develop a schema where victory, resilience, and elegance are associated with how the club plays. A fan's mental framework becomes a lens through which they view each match, strengthening their connection to the team, and in the process, permanently transforming how they think and act in the world as well.[2]

Schemas aren't only used by fans to interpret sport performances. They also shape the emotional responses and beliefs fans carry forward, even after the games have ended. In places like Santiago, Chile, where many fans passionately support Colo-Colo football club, and Japan, where baseball is prized as a national pastime, schemas provide fans with a framework to experience and interpret sports as immutable parts of their personal lives. This chapter investigates how cognitive structures – the ways fans think – support sports faith. It reveals how fans develop deeply founded loyalty and belief systems, often transcending logic or reason, through the shared language of sports.

THE MIND AS A REPOSITORY FOR SPORTS

Fans first observe sports and teams but then their minds translate them into schemas incorporating existing symbols, memories, and meanings so that sport becomes intertwined with a fan's mental processes. A fan's cognitive repository therefore holds representations of players, teams, and defining moments, creating a mental landscape that embeds sports content into a fan's thinking process.[3] In a crude sense, fans think with and through sports. For example, a fan of Kenyan distance running might picture Kelvin Kiptum's victory at the 2023 Chicago Marathon, where he set the world record, as the epitome of human endurance and mental strength. However, the moment isn't just a record in a database, but a symbol of the fortitude and pride deeply embedded in Kenya's running culture because it's deeply etched in the minds of Kenyan fans. For such fans, thinking about running is inseparable from thinking about Kiptum.

Schemas are central to allegiance because they act as mental templates that help fans organize and interpret sports events. They make it possible for a fan to recognize and react to familiar patterns, like an American football fan who instinctively feels heightened anticipation before a fourth down and goal attempt. Each experience – whether a now-famous match, a celebrated play, or even an iconic logo – adds layers to these schemas, helping fans process new moments with immediate familiarity and a sharpened emotional response. Consider a young fan in Australia watching the Matildas, Australia's national women's soccer (football) team. The mental image of a favorite player becomes part of the fan's schema for excellence and aspiration. It's an indelible mental imprint that regulates how fans perceive the world and their place within it. Cognitive schemas connect fans to sports properties of cultural and personal significance. In Italy, where football reigns supreme, a Juventus fan might recall iconic goals by Alessandro Del Piero, embellishing the belief that skill and loyalty define their team's identity. Across the Atlantic in the United States, Chicago Bulls basketball fans still deify Michael Jordan's winning shot in the 1998 NBA finals as a symbol of mastery under pressure. Mental schemas, or 'schemata', allow these moments to resonate, guiding fans in how they interpret forthcoming games and seasons to come.

As schemas build over time, they also become culturally embedded, connecting individuals to the broader fan community. In Buenos Aires, for example, River Plate football fans view themselves as part of a larger story involving traditions including legendary players, historic wins, and unforgettable rivalries. Each match serves as a ritualistic reaffirmation of what they believe their team stands for.[4] In Japan, baseball fans bring a similar reverence to the game, recalling the accomplishments of players like Sadaharu Oh and the team pride associated with the Hanshin Tigers or Yomiuri Giants. Fans' schemas create emotional 'anchors' that shape how they decode every aspect of the sport, strengthening their faith in their teams and athletes, game after game. The fact is that no fan recalls objective facts about their sports or teams. At best it's a messy pastiche of sensory recollections, shadowy fragments, and post-event rationalizations, all soaked in emotional sweat.

Sports fandom connects community and shared experience to individual emotions. The thrill of a game-winning goal, the despair of a last-second loss, and the joy of a championship victory are all emotional moments amplified by the presence of fellow fans and made more meaningful by the collective experience. In stadiums, living rooms, and public squares, people gather to experience the game together, creating emotional bonds that extend beyond common sporting allegiance. Picture the passionate supporters of the Golden State Warriors in San Francisco, who rally around their team in moments of both victory and defeat, or the waves of fans chanting in Tokyo's baseball stadiums as the Yomiuri Giants take the field. These shared emotions foster a sense of unity, making fans feel part of something larger than themselves. Belonging constitutes a key component of sports fans' faith in their teams, and a pivotal amplifier of emotional volume.[5]

Emotional connections can resonate through social contexts too, like in women's sports where fans might see their support as a statement of equality and empowerment. The success of the United States Women's national soccer team has inspired a dedicated following, with fans rallying not only around the athletes' skill but also around their role as champions of gender equity in sports. When Megan Rapinoe, for example, scored a goal, it was not just a victory on the field; it was a moment of empowerment for millions who looked up to her as a leader both on and off the field. Similarly, some fans of the WNBA view their support as part of a broader movement, seeing each game as a step toward more visibility and support for women's sports.

Fans of para sports, too, find deep meaning in their connection to athletes who overcome challenges to compete at the highest level. The Paralympic Games are filled with stories of athletes who redefine the limits of physical ability, and fans who cheer for them can see these moments as symbols of inclusion and achievement. In watching a wheelchair basketball game or a visually impaired sprinter, fans can experience a strong emotional resonance at least in part because the achievement of sporting mastery seems greater. These shared emotional experiences create a sense of pride that transcends the specific outcome of any event, solidifying fans' faith in the broader values of the sport. In these moments, sports faith is about more than just team loyalty, but also about solidarity, pride, and belonging.

BELIEFS AND FAITH IN SPORTS

The beliefs that fans hold about their teams, athletes, and sports are complex and interwoven with individual experiences, cultural backgrounds, and a network of shared stories and symbols. Yet fan beliefs serve as a framework that allows them to make sense of the ups and downs of sports, adding a layer of meaning to each victory and defeat.[6] For instance, a Manchester United fan might see every comeback win as proof of their team's indomitable spirit, while a Japanese sumo fan may interpret their favorite rikishi's success as a confirmation of discipline and honor, values deeply embedded in the culture. Beliefs shape how fans experience games, guiding their responses to each new event in the sports world.

As sport beliefs deepen, they turn into a more profound emotional commitment: faith. Sports faith is a mental and emotional loyalty that persists despite challenges, losses, and disappointments.[7] Faithful beliefs in sports can mirror broader social values, giving fans a way to express their principles through support. As noted earlier, fans of women's soccer, for example, might see their loyalty as part of a movement for gender equity, celebrating the achievements of players as symbols of progress and empowerment. The increasing popularity of the Women's Super League in England, where fans support teams like Arsenal and Chelsea, is seen by many as a step toward a more inclusive and equal sporting world. Fans don't just follow a team but contribute to a cultural shift, celebrating the growing visibility and success of women's sports.

For many fans, team beliefs form the foundation of their sports faith, offering a way to find meaning and identity in every game. Sports fandom thereby becomes a way to align with values and ideals that resonate most. For example, fans of the Brazilian national football team don't just cheer for the players, they celebrate the legacy of 'samba football', a style that embodies creativity, flair, and freedom on the field. The belief in a national playing style becomes a source of identity for fans, who see Brazil's achievements as an affirmation of cultural values beyond football. As fans solidify their team beliefs into faith, they can transcend the immediate success or failure of their teams. Sports faith is a powerful form of commitment, where loyalty remains constant even through challenging times. In Scotland, fans of Celtic FC view their allegiance as a defining part of their heritage, with each game a ritual that reinforces their identity and the community bonds they prioritize. Such faith endures even when victories are few, as supporters continue to hold tight to the shared values and memories they associate with the club. Similarly, fans of the Chicago Cubs remained devoted through decades of defeat, waiting over a century for a World Series win in 2016. For these fans, the long journey of support made the victory more meaningful, a testament to enduring loyalty and to their faith.

Faithful beliefs operate as enduring structures that fans draw upon to make sense of the sports world. Through them fans find a powerful connection to their teams that carries them through wins, losses, and everything in between. In short, beliefs help fans understand the world by providing an interpretive lens; a way of making sense of it all. Collectively, they sort the wheat from the chaff and give fans a basis for making decisions and acting. As neuroscientific research connecting thinking and emotions has shown, faithful beliefs also allow fans to turn inwards, giving structure to identity, and feedback on the assumptions they make about themselves. The process is mediated by sport schemas embedded in memories colored by emotion.

MEMORY AND PERCEPTION IN SPORTS FANDOM

Memory is central to how fans experience and interpret sports, shaping beliefs and reinforcing sports faith. Memorable moments on the field are etched into the minds of fans, becoming emotional reference points that define how they view each new performance, game, and season. The most salient memories go beyond simple recollections. They are filled with significance, capturing the highs, lows, and pivotal moments that give sport its sense of drama and meaning. A German football fan, for instance, might remember Mario Götze's decisive goal in the 2014 FIFA World Cup final. However, memory is selective, and fans' recollections are likely to emphasize moments that align with their beliefs, while minimizing those that don't. Selective recall helps maintain fans' optimistic outlook on their teams and keeps their faith intact. Consider a fan of the United States women's national soccer team. They might vividly recall the thrilling penalty shootout in the 1999 FIFA World Cup final when Brandi Chastain scored the winning goal against China. The moment is remembered as a symbol of American excellence and as a breakthrough for women's sports, even as other, less favorable memories might fade into the background, like the outcome of the 2023 event. In this way, selective memory helps fans focus on the positive aspects of sports, preserving the emotional investment that keeps them engaged season after season.

While the selective memory process involves recalling past events, it also influences how fans perceive new ones. For example, a basketball fan in Canada may think back to the Toronto Raptors' championship victory in 2019 and, as a result, may interpret a close playoff game the following season with the same excitement, seeing each shot and rebound as carrying similar weight. Memory weaves past emotions into the present, giving fans a basis for emotional responses that feel immediate, regardless of when the original events occurred.

Perception also plays a role in how fans make sense of sports moments, allowing them to focus on specific aspects that reinforce their beliefs. A supporter of adaptive sports or para sports might view each race or match not only as a contest but as a testament to the athletes' determination, focusing on how they overcome unique challenges. Perception allows fans to emphasize the athletes' perseverance over any limitations they may face. It reinforces a positive narrative that affirms faith in the sports, teams, and athletes. By focusing on the aspects that resonate with their values, fans strengthen their emotional connection to sports, seeing it as a reflection of deeper beliefs and ideals.

Memory and perception work together to sustain fans' faith in their teams and athletes, helping them process both victories and defeats in ways that align with their sports schemas. A Liverpool FC fan, for example, might perceive each comeback win as part of the club's long history of resilience, remembering iconic moments like the 2005 UEFA Champions League final when Liverpool overcame a 3–0 halftime deficit to win against AC Milan. Memories become normalized too, shaping the fan expectations of current games as opportunities for yet another dramatic comeback. Memory therefore becomes part of the mental scaffolding that supports sports faith, providing fans with a foundation upon which they build their beliefs and maintain their loyalty.

SHORTCUTS TO SPORTS BELIEFS

To navigate the high-stakes, fast-paced world of sports, fans rely on heuristics, which are thinking shortcuts that simplify complex choices into manageable options. Heuristics assist fans to process vast amounts of information rapidly, giving them a sense of consistency in how they decipher game events, controversies, and outcomes. Consider a fan of the Brazilian national football team that I mentioned earlier. They might rely on the heuristic that 'Brazilian football is all about skill and flair', a belief that colors how they interpret every pass, goal, and performance. Mental shortcuts reinforce expectations for each game, allowing the fan to experience each match as a verification of the team's style and identity.

Heuristics also play a significant role in the perseverance of sports beliefs because they bolster fans' faith in teams, players, and even specific play styles despite disappointing results or controversial decisions. Imagine a Tongan rugby fan who believes in the rough and rugged nature of their team's playing style. When faced with a loss, they might attribute it to unfavorable refereeing or bad weather rather than flaws in the team's strategy or skills.[8] Cognitive shortcuts help the fan remain loyal to the team's style and traditions, rather than viewing each setback as a reason to question their faith.

Belief frameworks incorporate heuristics so that fans can focus on the positive aspects of each game, maintaining a steady sense of admiration and emotional investment, regardless of outcomes. Mental shortcuts therefore serve as psychological defenses, protecting fans from the disillusionment that might otherwise come with losses or disappointing performances. For instance, when fans of historically successful teams like the Korean Taekwondo team face a difficult Olympics or world championship, they might lean on heuristics like 'It's just a rebuilding period' or 'We always come back stronger' to help them cope with the temporary setback. Heuristics simplify complex scenarios and protect the emotional investment fans place in their teams. They provide a reliable framework for processing the ups and downs that come with sports loyalty, and for navigating moments of turbulence or unpredictability, as they give fans a way to reframe unfavorable situations without reevaluating their core beliefs.

Through heuristics, fans gain a set of cognitive 'guardrails' that stabilize their beliefs, making it easier to navigate the volatile nature of sports. Whether it's excusing a loss, rationalizing a team's struggles, or celebrating a comeback, heuristics ensure that fans can maintain a consistent and faithful outlook on their teams, even in the face of setbacks. Psychologists refer to the practice of fiercely guarding deeply held beliefs as a central feature of the 'psychological immune system'. Ideas and information that threaten a fan's core sport beliefs will be challenged, disparaged, undermined, vilified, and rejected to avoid any uncomfortable truths challenging their comfortable faith-cemented illusions. Since the mind's belief immune system works unconsciously, fans do not intentionally delude themselves or conspire to undermine unnerving ideas. Mostly, fans remain oblivious to their mind's protective conniving, which helpfully quashes any incoming information that could lead to stress, anxiety, distress, and worst of all, contradiction about how they view themselves or their beloved sports teams or players.[9]

SPORT BELIEFS AS SUPERORDINATE IDEOLOGIES

Sports beliefs might begin as preferences or pastimes, but they rise to the level of 'superordinate ideologies', anchoring fans' identities in ways that are profound and unwavering. This level of belief transforms a fan's connection to a team or athlete into a core part of who they are, comparable to deeply held values or cultural identities. Supporting a team becomes a commitment, and the team's success or failure feels like a personal victory or defeat. The phenomenon is evident in fan cultures around the world, where allegiance to a club or athlete represents a form of identity. Many fans develop extreme attitudes, and some of these coalesce into rigid beliefs. Extreme attitudes and beliefs demand uncompromising adherence, subordinating other aspects of life and the beliefs attached to them including family, friends, work, or leisure.[10] For this reason, I label such powerful beliefs as superordinate.

In Argentina, for example, fans of Boca Juniors are supporters, but they also identify as part of a 'Boca family'. Each match becomes a ritual reinforcing their place within the Boca community, which extends through neighborhoods, generations, and entire social groups. Boca Juniors fans proudly display the club's colors wherever they go. They experience the team's successes as personal victories and its losses as acutely felt setbacks. Faith in the team means that their devotion is part of a superordinate belief where the game itself is just one component in a shared identity that ties individuals to their community and to each other.[11]

When sports beliefs reach a superordinate level, they become extremely resilient, withstanding losses, controversies, and changes within the team. For example, as I've mentioned, in Scotland, fans of Celtic FC view their connection to the club as an intractable part of their heritage. The team's history and significance in Scottish communities are embedded in the fan experience, turning each match into a reaffirmation of shared identity and cultural pride. Even during difficult seasons, Celtic fans continue to rally around their team, seeing each game as an expression of the values and traditions they revere. Superordinate beliefs in sports are therefore more than just attachments to a team. They are expressions of loyalty to a way of life or a set of values. Fans remain committed, even through downturns, because their faith is tied to something much larger than a score.[12]

Ultimately, superordinate beliefs in sports serve as a psychological foundation, grounding fans in identities that feel stable and meaningful, regardless of external circumstances. By tying their sports faith to core values or cultural heritage, fans create lasting connections that go beyond the immediacy of the game, enriching their lives and creating communities united by shared beliefs.

COGNITIVE FLEXIBILITY IN SPORTS FAN PSYCHOLOGY

While many sports beliefs are deeply ingrained, most fans also display cognitive flexibility, which means that they can adjust their perspectives and expectations in response to changing circumstances. Cognitive flexibility is a form of mental adaptability that lets fans balance loyalty with openness, making it possible to enjoy sports from multiple angles. For example, a French football fan might have a fierce loyalty to Paris Saint-Germain (PSG) during the domestic season but shift gears to cheer on the national team, 'Les Bleus', during international tournaments like the FIFA World Cup. Mental 'switching' explains how fans can hold layered loyalties, honoring both club and country, or supporting club teams in more than one sport.

Mental flexibility can be geographical but may also apply to different teams, sports, and leagues. A cricket fan in Australia might be devoted to the national team during international test matches but also feel a strong connection to one of their city's Twenty20 Big Bash League (BBL) teams, appreciating the unique style of play each setting brings. Similarly, fans of the NBA might follow a specific home team, such as the Los Angeles Lakers, while also admiring the skill of players from other teams, such as Giannis Antetokounmpo or Steph Curry. An openness to celebrating talent outside their primary fandom reflects cognitive flexibility where fans recognize excellence across different contexts without feeling that they're compromising their core loyalties.

Cognitive flexibility enables fans to navigate social changes within sports. For example, as women's sports gain visibility and popularity, traditional fans of men's leagues increasingly support women's teams, embracing the value women bring to the sports world. Basketball fans who have long followed the NBA are now showing enthusiasm for the WNBA, supporting players like Breanna Stewart and A'ja Wilson with the same level of dedication. Similarly, the capacity to adapt helps fans traverse generational transitions within teams. Fans of the German national football team might have admired players like Miroslav Klose and Philipp Lahm, but as those stars retired, fans embraced new talents like Joshua Kimmich and Kai Havertz, understanding that the team's legacy is as much about the future as it is about the past. Cognitive flexibility keeps fans faithful to their teams while welcoming new players and evolving dynamics. As a result, fans keep their sports faith intact through the inevitable changes that occur over time. Cognitive adaptability enriches the sports experience for fans.

GLOBAL NATURE OF SPORTS FAITH

Sports faith is a universal experience, bridging cultural, geographic, and social divides to create a shared human bond. Around the world, sports act as a common language, allowing fans to connect through values like perseverance, teamwork, and pride. Whether it's in the stadiums of South America, the football fields of Africa, or the basketball courts of Southeast Asia, sports have a unique power to unite people, providing a sense of belonging that transcends borders. Fans gather, often wearing the colors of their teams, chanting and celebrating as one, showcasing the universal appeal of sports.

International events like the Olympics, the Paralympics, and the FIFA World Cup are prime examples of this global unity. During these competitions, athletes from around the world compete not only for medals but to represent their countries, cultures, and ideals. The Paralympics, for example, highlights how sports can unite people across differences, as fans rally behind athletes who challenge conventional definitions of performance. Global moments create lasting memories that foster connections across cultures. For instance, the 1995 Rugby World Cup in South Africa symbolized the country's post-apartheid unity. South Africans of all backgrounds rallied behind their team, and the image of Nelson Mandela presenting the trophy to the captain, Francois Pienaar, became a symbol of reconciliation and national pride. The event resonated with South Africans but also moved fans around the world. Emotional content in sports can bring people together in powerful, symbolic ways.

Sports faith on a global scale is further evident in the solidarity seen among fans of women's football. The growth of the FIFA Women's World Cup has led to a surge in global support, with fans cheering for teams from countries like Brazil, the United States, Japan, and Nigeria. The excitement around foundational players like Marta Vieira da Silva, Megan Rapinoe, and Sam Kerr helped women's football reach new audiences, creating a new fan base and reflecting a broader cultural shift. In parts of Africa, sport is a source of inspiration and ambition. Young athletes and players in Nigeria or Kenya dream of emulating their heroes like Nwankwo Kanu or Eliud Kipchoge, to use sports as a pathway to new opportunities. For fans in these communities, cheering for local athletes or following international stars provides a sense of pride and collective identity, reinforcing their belief in the potential of sports to change lives. Sports faith is as much a global phenomenon as it is personal. From raucous stadiums in Argentina to the crowded basketball courts of the Philippines, fans around the world engage with sports as a shared journey, celebrating achievements, enduring losses, and finding meaning in the collective experience.

INTEGRATING THE PSYCHOLOGY OF
SPORTS FAITH

As I noted at the outset of the chapter, the mind organizes past experiences into schemas or cognitive structures that subsequently work to interpret new experiences based on prior knowledge. In sports fandom, schemas become embedded mental frameworks that define how fans process wins, losses, and defining moments in a way that builds lasting loyalty. A fan of competitive fencing, for example, may associate agility, honor, and precision with the sport. Over time, each match, touché, or controversial call reinforces this schema, strengthening the fan's emotional investment in these values. Schemas also serve as templates for emotional and behavioral responses. A fan of mixed martial arts may learn to appreciate power and strategy, associating these values with the sport's icons. Schemas extend beyond the game itself, affecting fans' outlook on challenges and conflict in daily life. The intense focus required in archery, the patience celebrated in fly-fishing, or the adaptability needed in esports are not just game skills but cognitive and emotional anchors that fans carry into their worlds.

The experience of sports faith is then amplified by communities. The excitement of witnessing a masterful sailing maneuver or a decisive judo 'ippon' is heightened in the presence of fellow enthusiasts. Whether in the stadium, at home, or in online forums, fans share in the highs and lows, creating bonds that deepen their connection to each other and to their chosen sports. In niche sports like bouldering or ultimate frisbee, community bonds are especially significant. These sports often attract dedicated followers who find meaning not just in the sport but in the camaraderie it fosters. The connection fans feel toward athletes overcoming obstacles reflects their own shared challenges, fostering a sense of solidarity fused through a common belief framework.

Beliefs held by fans about their teams, athletes, or sport serve as interpretive frameworks, infusing each game with resonance. For instance, a rock-climbing enthusiast may see each ascent as a symbol of respect for nature, mirroring personal values that guide their lives outside of the sport. As these beliefs gain traction, they form into sports faith that operates as a psychological and emotional commitment that endures through both triumphs and failures. A fan of women's boxing may celebrate the sport's culture of empowerment, seeing each win or loss as part of a broader struggle for equality and self-expression. This type of belief can transform sports into platforms for advocating change, celebrating inclusion, and redefining societal norms. It also lingers in memory as decisive anchors attached to certain fan behaviors. Memory is therefore a central component in how fans experience and interpret sports. It turns peak moments into lasting emotional touchstones that influence future experiences.

The most salient memories are rarely objective. Instead, they are shaped by selective recall, emphasizing moments that align with the fan's beliefs and values. For example, in 2016, Eddie Hall made history by lifting a world-record 500 kg (1,102 lbs) in a deadlift at the World Deadlift Championships in Leeds. After the lift, Hall collapsed to the floor, momentarily blacking out from the excruciating exertion. Fans of the World's Strongest Man competitor may recall the triumphant lift as an unparalleled exemplification of personal power and achievement. Memory works alongside perception to shape how fans interpret new moments. A biathlon enthusiast may recall a heartstopping final shot and transfer that thrill to future competitions, viewing each subsequent race through the same intense emotional lens. Selective memory thus creates a cognitive scaffolding that bolsters faith, guiding how fans recall past events and frame future ones.

To process the fast-paced, high-stakes world of sports, fans rely on heuristics, which simplify complex events into manageable ideas. For example, a sumo wrestling fan might hold the heuristic that 'strength and honor always prevail', which helps them interpret every match through this ideal, regardless of outcome. Heuristics consequently play a key role in maintaining belief resilience, especially in the face of unexpected outcomes or unfavorable calls. A fan of endurance team road cycling might rationalize a loss due to uncontrollable factors like weather or course conditions, rather than questioning the team's strategies or skill. This mental shortcut enables fans to remain loyal to their beliefs, buffering their emotional investment from external challenges.

What begins as a simple attachment to a team or athlete can evolve into a superordinate ideology, anchoring a fan's identity in ways comparable to cultural values or personal philosophies. Take the fans of the annual Iditarod sled dog race in Alaska. Their devotion to the event embodies a deep respect for wilderness survival and endurance. Fans see each race as a celebration of nature's challenges and human resilience, binding them to values that transcend the race itself. In martial arts like Brazilian jiu-jitsu, fans and practitioners may regard their training and support as a lifestyle, where the sport's philosophy of 'gentle art' and mental discipline becomes integral to their sense of self. Such a level of belief, or what I've termed superordinate, is resilient and remains steadfast even amid challenges. Fans' faith is cemented in values that go beyond individual matches or athletes.

Despite unbending beliefs, many fans also exhibit cognitive flexibility, adjusting perspectives and loyalties in response to new contexts. For instance, a fan of sandboarding might also support skateboarding or snowboarding athletes, appreciating the shared skillset while remaining loyal to their original sport. Cognitive flexibility allows fans to navigate different sports while maintaining core loyalties, expanding their appreciation without compromising their original commitments. Adaptability is seen in fans who embrace multiple formats, such as those who support both traditional football and the growing sport of futsal. Cognitive flexibility thus enriches fandom, allowing fans to celebrate talent and dedication across various contexts while staying connected to the unique identity of each sport. Sports faith is a universal language that connects people across cultures and continents.

CONCLUSION: FAITH AND FEELING

The psychology of sports faith reveals how the human mind creates meaning, identity, and belonging through sports, crafting a powerful narrative that goes beyond the immediate thrill of the game. Sports serve as an emotional and psychological anchor, providing fans with a sense of purpose, connection, and pride. Faith binds fans of all ages, abilities, and backgrounds, allowing them to celebrate victories and endure losses with unwavering loyalty. Some fans develop extreme attitudes, and some of these coalesce into rigid beliefs. Extreme attitudes and beliefs demand uncompromising adherence, subordinating other aspects of life and the beliefs attached to them including family, friends, work, or leisure.

Sports faith shapes how fans interpret not only the outcomes of games but also the stories that unfold around them. The joy of a miraculous comeback, the pride in a national team's success, and the heartbreak of an unexpected defeat, all form part of the mental landscape that fans carry with them, etched into their memories as chapters in a larger story. When fans invest in sports, they're participating in an ancient human tradition that reflects universal values of loyalty, resilience, and camaraderie.

Through sports, fans find an outlet for expressing core human emotions. A fan cheering for the underdog at the Paralympics feels the same rush of pride as a supporter celebrating their team's championship win. In both cases, fans engage in a shared emotional experience that unites them with others, building connections that transcend language, culture, and geography. This ability to evoke intense emotions is one of sport's most enduring qualities. Sport delivers a source of joy, solace, and even healing for millions of fans. The universal appeal of sports faith illustrates its role as both a personal and collective expression of what it means to be human. The collision of cognitive processes, cultural symbols, and emotional responses produces a potent mixture that makes sport one of humanity's most persistent passions. Fans don't just support a team. They believe in it. They have faith in it. They believe in the athletes who represent them, in the colors they wear, and in the history they honor. Through this faith, fans create a sense of identity that endures for a lifetime and delivers endless emotional highs and lows. It is to a more detailed elaboration of emotion that we now turn.

NOTES

1 Dwyer, B., Slavich, M. A., & Gellock, J. L. (2018). A fan's search for meaning: Testing the dimensionality of sport fan superstition. *Sport Management Review*, 21(5), 533–548.

2 Hirt, E. R., Clarkson, J. J., & Zillmann, D. (2021). The psychology of sports fanship: Emotional and cognitive aspects. *Journal of Sport & Exercise Psychology*, 43(3), 245–260.

3 Connors, M. H., & Halligan, P. W. (2015). A cognitive account of belief: A tentative road map. *Frontiers in Psychology*, 5, 1–14.

4 D'Acremont, M., Schultz, W., & Bossaerts, P. (2013). The human brain encodes event frequencies while forming subjective beliefs. *Journal of Neuroscience*, 33(26), 10887–10897.

5 Kerr, J. H., & Gladden, J. M. (2021). Emotion in sports fans: The role of excitement and stress. *International Review of Sport and Exercise Psychology*, 14(2), 244–263.

6 Damasio, A. R. (2000). Thinking about belief. In D. L. Schacter & E. Scarry (Eds.), *Memory, brain and belief* (pp. 325–334). Harvard University Press.

7 Wann, D. L., & Weaver, S. (2020). Understanding sport fan aggression: The role of identification and emotional investment. *Journal of Applied Social Psychology*, 50(4), 211–225.

8 Erikstad, M. K., & Johansen, B. T. (2020). Referee bias in professional football: Favoritism toward successful teams in potential penalty situations. *Frontiers in Sports and Active Living*, 2, 19.

9 Duarte, I. C., Afonso, S., Jorge, H., Cayolla, R., Ferreira, C., & Castelo-Branco, M. (2017). Tribal love: The neural correlates of passionate engagement in football fans. *Social Cognitive and Affective Neuroscience*, 12(5), 718–728.

10 Decety, J., Pape, R., & Workman, C. I. (2018). A multilevel social neuroscience perspective on radicalization and terrorism. *Social Neuroscience*, 13(5), 511–529.

11 Branscombe, N. R., & Wann, D. L. (2020). Collective self-esteem consequences of fan identification. *Journal of Sport & Exercise Psychology*, 27(5), 546–557.

12 Choi, J.-K., & Bowles, S. (2007). The coevolution of parochial altruism and war. *Science*, 318(5850), 636–640.

3

THE PSYCHOLOGY OF SPORTS EMOTIONS

INTRODUCTION: MINDSETS AND MECHANISMS

In this chapter, I venture further into the psychological mechanisms that fuel fervent sports fandom, building on the concepts from the previous chapter, which established that belief and faith in sports and teams taps into fans' needs for identity, connection, and meaning. I also develop a stronger connection between the mind's evolutionary legacy and fan psychology. While leaping away from a shadow that resembles a predator or recognizing the face of a friend in a crowd might seem unrelated to sports fandom, these instincts reveal how our minds are naturally primed to stimulate action and feeling without conscious thought.

The chapter introduces four key cognitive mechanisms that make fans more receptive to sports and explains how these mental processes make fandom an enduring and emotionally charged experience.[1] First, the ability to develop 'theories of mind' allows fans to empathize with fellow supporters, players, and athletes, sharing in their joys and sorrows. Second, fans exercise a powerful mental capacity to mimic and replicate behaviors, helping fan culture spread like wildfire across generations and regions. Third, memory is biased toward emotionally significant events, making sports victories and defeats stand out

DOI: 10.4324/9781003587699-3

in fans' minds for lifetimes. Lastly, the intertwining of thought and emotion makes it easy for fans to invest emotionally in their teams, creating a kind of loyalty that is resistant to logical reasoning. We start with mind reading and work our way toward a full account of how all four mechanisms integrate with emotions to deliver compelling experiences.

MIND-READING ATHLETES

One of the foundational mental abilities that supports fan experiences is known as 'theory of mind', which is the capacity to understand and predict the thoughts and feelings of others. Developed in early childhood, the skill is essential for interpreting the intentions and emotions of others, even without direct information about what they're thinking. Theory of mind allows fans to make sense of complex social interactions, including the intricate dynamics in the world of sports. Imagine, for example, watching an Olympic gymnast like Simone Biles perform a high-stakes routine. In those breathtaking moments, fans find themselves empathizing with her focus, her calculated movements, and her poise under pressure. Even if a fan has never performed a gymnastics routine, their brains can fabricate her imagined emotions, impelling them to feel her tension, celebrate her triumphs, and even experience disappointment if something goes wrong.[2]

The innate mental capacity to imagine the experience of athletes extends beyond the observation of elite competition. Local fans in a stadium supporting their home team feel a sense of comradeship based on the assumption that they understand each other's shared excitement, anxiety, and frustration.[3] In Japanese baseball, fans are known for their coordinated chants and cheers that enhance the atmosphere of each game. The sense of shared emotion helps create a stronger bond among fans, as though each fan understands the minds of others in their cheering section. Feelings of community and shared understanding heightens fans' collective experience, creating belonging and powerful rituals.[4] Similarly, fans' theory of mind extends to how they react to players, referees, and the game dynamics. When something goes wrong in a match, like a questionable penalty, for instance, fans quickly assign blame, often feeling as though the referee acted with some bias or intent to favor the other team. An attribution of agency to referees reflects the mind's tendency to see a biased intention behind actions.

Theory of mind bonds fans to each other and to players and athletes but also influences how they respond to unfavorable events. When a game doesn't go as expected, fans often feel a powerful need to make sense of the disappointment. Cricket fans are notoriously quick to criticize umpires or weather conditions that impact their team's performance. During the 2019 Cricket World Cup, England's controversial victory over New Zealand in the final, which was decided by boundary count, sparked an outcry among New Zealand fans, who felt the rules were unfair. Attributing blame can also fuel superstitions, a common aspect of fandom across cultures and sports. Superstitions offer a way for fans to feel a sense of control. Whether it's wearing a 'lucky hat' or performing a specific pre-game routine, fans use rituals to try to influence outcomes. For example, fans of Rafael Nadal know he has his own set of superstitions and pre-match rituals, which many fans then replicated in their own routines, hoping it would bring success to their idol. Such beliefs, however irrational, become a fundamental part of the fan experience, offering comfort and a sense of personal agency and relevance. We can now start to see how some of the fan behaviors that I introduced in earlier chapters can be partly explained by capacities like theory of mind. Going a step further, the ability to imagine agency also propels mimicry.

MIMICRY AND THE SPREAD OF FAN CULTURE

Beyond empathy, another cognitive mechanism that fuels sports fandom is the hardwired inclination to mimic and adopt observed behaviors. Psychologists refer to this tendency as 'social contagion'. It's especially prominent in sports, where fans adopt rituals, gestures, chants, and songs that they see other fans doing. Mimicry encourages fan traditions to spread across communities and generations, reinforcing the sense of belonging between fans. An example is found in Brazilian sporting culture, where fans sing chants and perform the samba to support their national teams. As shared actions, the cultural practices are passed down through generations, inculcating young fans. Similarly, fans of the New Zealand All Blacks rugby team mimic the team's famous 'haka', a traditional Māori war dance, to intimidate opponents and rally their own team before each match. Though fans may not perform the haka themselves, they often chant or celebrate it, adopting the emotional intensity and meaning behind it as part of their fan identity.

Mimicry spreads to behaviors that fans exhibit to fit in with fan culture. A young, novice fan might start by imitating how seasoned fans dress, speak, or cheer. That's why most tennis fans attending Wimbledon adopt the traditional attire and etiquette of the event, dressing in a style that aligns with the tournament's reputation for elegance and tradition. In tennis, the tradition of bowing or curtsying to the royal box at Wimbledon adds a layer of formal respect and ritual to the game as well. Fans who attend Wimbledon are expected to dress in smart attire, respecting the tournament's legacy and creating a unique atmosphere. New fans mimic these practices, not just to fit in, but to feel part of the tradition and heritage of Wimbledon. Such mimicry reinforces a fan's emotional connection to the sport, making the experience more meaningful.[5]

In cricket, young fans in India emulate the cricketing style and attitude of their favorite players like Virat Kohli or Smriti Mandhana, and they watch games with the same intensity and focus as older fans around them. Mimicry helps novice fans feel accepted, making it more likely they will continue their fandom. By copying others, fans feel a sense of belonging while reinforcing their emotional investment in the team. Social mimicry solidifies the bonds within fan communities, creating an atmosphere where everyone's reactions – from joy to frustration – are synchronized. When fans feel like part of a larger group, their emotional highs and lows feel amplified, creating a rewarding experience that keeps them coming back.

Social contagion also plays a role in the rituals that fans adopt. In the world of motorsports, particularly Formula 1, fans show loyalty to specific teams, such as Ferrari or Mercedes, often dressing in the team's colors. In the same vein, during the cricket World Cup, fans from different nations paint their faces, dress up in national colors, and mimic chants and dances seen in past tournaments. Rituals further embed emotions into the fan experience due to their memorability.

MEMORY AND EMOTION IN SPORTS FANDOM

I introduced memory in the last chapter, signaling its importance in how fans think about the targets of their sporting commitment. One of the most fascinating aspects of sports fandom is how well fans remember specific games, moments, and even minor details about matches that took place a long time ago. It's because brains are wired to retain emotionally charged events with vivid detail. The intensity of emotions felt during a game strengthens fans' memories of it, which is why they can often recall a particular play or game with remarkable clarity. Today, middle-aged American fans of the 'Miracle on Ice' game, where the U.S. men's ice hockey team defeated the heavily favored Soviet Union in the 1980 Winter Olympics, can report in detail the feelings they experienced watching the game as a child. Similarly, more recently, fans of the Nigerian women's national football team remember the team's triumph at the 2018 Africa Women Cup of Nations, when Nigeria emerged victorious after a dramatic final against South Africa.

Fan memories of intense sports moments are further strengthened through social reinforcement. When fans talk to each other about the unforgettable moments from a game, they re-experience the emotions, reinforcing the memory. In Argentina, for instance, fans continue to celebrate and debate Diego Maradona's 'Hand of God' goal against England from the 1986 FIFA World Cup. Each retelling of that iconic moment – the skill, the controversy, and the triumph – reinvigorates the memory for both those who were present and those who have heard about it through others. England fans speak passionately about it too, but with remarkably enduring fury. In addition, poignant events can become embedded in the collective fan memory, such as Naomi Osaka's 2020 U.S. Open win, where she wore a mask with the names of Black victims of police violence to highlight the social issue. Her victory was more than a sports accomplishment; it became a moment of cultural significance, blending memory, emotion, and activism in ways that resonated with fans worldwide.

The tendency to recall specific sports moments vividly illustrates the interplay of memory and emotion. When fans witness something extraordinary, the concentrated emotions make the memory difficult to forget. Should memories become further laden with social and cultural meaning, they assume part of the fan's identity, transforming sports from a pastime into a vital part of personal character and augmenting an emotional commitment to fandom.

Sports are unique in how they blend thought and feeling, making fandom an emotionally charged experience. Beyond the thrill of a close game, fans form attachments to teams and players, creating a personal and enduring connection. The more a fan identifies with a team or athlete, the more they are willing to invest emotionally. Consider fans of former tennis great Serena Williams, who admire her not only for her athletic talent but also for her resilience, character, and role as a social agent. Williams' achievements on the tennis court are inspirational to millions, especially young women around the world, who see her as a trailblazer in a sport that has historically been limited in diversity. Fans feel a strong connection to Serena's journey, viewing her triumphs and setbacks as part of a shared story.

Emotional investment also explains why fans remain loyal even when their team underperforms or goes through extended losing streaks. Take, for instance, the Scottish national football team, which has had a challenging history in international competitions. Despite the lack of major international success, Scottish fans are famously passionate and fiercely devoted. They fill stadiums, travel for away games, and celebrate even the smallest victories with unrestrained enthusiasm. In Japan, fans of sumo wrestling display a similar emotional commitment. As I mentioned in the previous chapter, supporting a favorite rikishi is a connection to Japan's ancient culture, values of discipline, and honor. Emotional commitment can lead fans to excuse failures and forgive lapses, focusing on the overarching loyalty rather than momentary setbacks. In the world of baseball, the Chicago Cubs exemplify this phenomenon. Before their historic 2016 World Series win, the Cubs had endured a 108-year championship drought. Yet, throughout those years, Cubs fans continued to support their team with unwavering dedication, famously embracing the identity of being 'lovable losers'.

BIAS, RATINGS, AND EVALUATIONS

I raised the importance of cognitive biases in the previous chapters, and now as we venture further into the psychology of sports fandom, it's instructive to explain how cognitive biases shape fans' emotions, as well as their perceptions and judgments of players, teams, and events. Minds are programmed to create shortcuts in processing information, leading fans to form rapid evaluations based on a mix of instinct and selective reasoning.[6] Mental shortcuts help fans make decisions quickly, but they also introduce biases that skew their opinions, especially when it comes to assessing favorite teams or athletes. Fans often believe that their judgments about a team's performance are fair and objective, but studies show that cognitive biases influence how fans evaluate almost everything in sports.[7] Whether it's rating a player's performance, assessing a referee's call, or comparing a favored team to a despised rival, fans' evaluations are rarely impartial. Here I explore several types of biases that influence fans' perceptions and examine how skewed mental habits shape the emotional character of sports fandom.[8]

HALO EFFECT

One of the most pervasive biases in sports fandom is the 'halo effect', where positive feelings toward a team or player influence how fans construe on-field behaviors. If a fan already likes or admires a player, they are more likely to view everything the player does in a positive light. The effect extends beyond individual athletes to entire teams, particularly those with legendary status or high-profile histories. Consider the reverence around Michael Jordan, widely considered one of the greatest basketball players in history. For Chicago Bulls fans and basketball enthusiasts, Jordan's reputation casts a positive halo over his actions both on and off the court. A halo effect means fans are more inclined to evaluate his decisions and actions generously, even if they might be critical of similar actions by other players. Likewise, the same bias can be seen with soccer superstars like Aitana Bonmatí, Marta, Lionel Messi, and Cristiano Ronaldo. Their devoted fans attribute their success to talent, hard work, and innate brilliance while downplaying or ignoring less favorable aspects of their careers, such as moments of frustration or errors on the field, as well as unsavory off-field transgressions.

Another common cognitive bias in sports fandom related to the halo effect is optimism bias, the tendency to expect positive outcomes despite poor past performance or realistic odds. Optimism bias helps explain why fans of perennial underdog teams continue to cheer with hope, regardless of past disappointments. For example, supporters of the Cleveland Browns in the NFL have endured numerous losing seasons, yet optimism persists year after year. Despite having never appeared in a Super Bowl, hope keeps Browns fans coming back, as they believe that the next season, game, or player acquisition could finally lead to success. Fans often view emerging stars with an implausibly optimistic lens too, projecting bright futures for young talents. The hype surrounding young stars like 2019 NBA first draft pick Zion Williamson or WNBA 2024 Rookie of the Year, Caitlin Clark, has fueled fan excitement, as they imagine these players breaking records and leading their teams to championships. Optimism bias shapes the fan narrative, creating a culture of expectation that can support athletes, but also creates pressure to live up to high hopes. Hope and optimism form part of the cognitive wiring that encourages fans to focus on potential positive outcomes rather than dwelling on the likelihood of failure, even if the latter is justified on past evidence and realistic probabilities.

FAMILIARITY BIAS

Familiarity bias is another powerful influence in sports, leading fans to favor players, teams, or leagues that are more well-known or widely covered in the media. It explains why fans tend to prefer major league teams over lesser-known teams, or why they support players who receive frequent media attention. Familiarity can create a sense of comfort and loyalty, encouraging fans to stick with certain teams or players rather than following lesser-known alternatives. Familiarity delivers a comfortable sense of emotional reassurance. For instance, tennis fans who watch major tournaments like Wimbledon or the U.S. Open are more familiar with top-ranked players like Jannik Sinner or Coco Gauff, which may lead them to prefer these players over other athletes. Familiarity bias shapes the viewing habits of fans, who may be more inclined to watch matches involving high-profile players while missing out on the excitement and talent found on the outer courts.

The bias also impacts sports media coverage, which tends to focus on well-established leagues and teams, reinforcing fans' preference for familiar entities. The popularity of the NBA, for instance, is partly a result of familiarity bias, as fans are continually exposed to star players and storylines. Conversely, lesser-known leagues, such as the Australian NBL or EuroLeague, attract far less attention, even though they showcase considerable talent and thrilling games. However, familiarity bias can create an intersection between comfort and loyalty. For example, baseball fans in Japan tend to support their home teams in the Nippon Professional Baseball league, such as the Hanshin

Tigers or Yomiuri Giants, forming deep attachments through repeated exposure to their games, players, and histories. Such regional loyalty reflects familiarity bias, as fans gravitate toward teams and players that feel like an extension of their community and identity, therefore providing emotional reassurance.

SIMILAR-TO-ME EFFECT

The 'similar-to-me' effect is another bias that influences sports fandom, where fans tend to rate players or teams more approvingly if they see aspects of themselves in them. It goes beyond regional or team-based loyalty and taps into the personal connection fans feel with athletes who share similar backgrounds, characteristics, or values. For instance, some Japanese football fans are drawn to players like Maya Yoshida and Takehiro Tomiyasu, who exemplify Japanese culture and values on the global stage. Similarly, young fans in South Korea feel a special pride in following Son Heung-min, whose success in the English Premier League has made him a national hero. Similarity connections strengthen fans' emotional investment, as they view some players as representatives of their own backgrounds and experiences. In the United States, the impact of representation is seen in basketball, where players like Stephen Curry and Klay Thompson inspire fans with their relatability and perceived humility. Curry's rise from a relatively unknown college player to an NBA superstar exemplifies the 'similar-to-me' effect for fans who admire his work ethic and feel a personal connection to his story as if they too could reach the top of the NBA.

ATTRACTIVENESS BIAS

Physical appearance can also influence fans' evaluations of athletes, creating a bias known as the 'attractiveness halo'. Athletes perceived as more attractive or taller are often rated higher by fans, even if their performance is similar, or even below, that of less attractive peers. It's especially prevalent in sports where visibility is high, such as basketball, tennis, and football, and it can affect both fan perception and marketing opportunities for players.

In football, for example, the attractiveness and athletic appearance of players like David Beckham or Alex Morgan can enhance their fan appeal, as their physical presence aligns with popular ideals of athleticism. In basketball, taller players such as Kevin Durant or Giannis Antetokounmpo receive greater attention, not just for their skills but because their height adds an element of visual dominance. Fans tend to unconsciously rate taller players as more dominant or capable, despite performance metrics that may not support the assumption. A preference for height and attractiveness also shapes the market-ability of players, as more 'attractive' or physically imposing athletes receive preferential sponsorships, advertisements, and endorsements. However, attractiveness bias can lead to skewed attention, with media focusing more on certain athletes based on appearance rather than performance, reflecting society's broader attractiveness biases, and perpetuating stereotypes and inequalities. Sports where bodies are on show, like swimming, beach volleyball, gymnastics, and diving, experience more physical stereotyping.

JUMPING TO CONCLUSIONS AND MOTIVATED REASONING

Another common cognitive-emotional response affecting sports fandom is the 'jump-to-conclusions' (JTC) bias, where fans quickly form strong opinions based on limited evidence. Fans make snap judgments about a player's performance or a team's season prospects based on a single game or play. JTC bias aligns with 'motivated reasoning', where fans perceive information in a way that supports their pre-existing beliefs or desired outcomes. Take, for example, fans' reactions to a rookie player's debut game. If the player performs excep-tionally well, fans might immediately assume they're a future super-star. Conversely, a poor debut may lead fans to prematurely assume that the player won't live up to expectations. A rush to judgment often occurs in highly competitive leagues like the NBA or EPL, where fans and analysts make hasty assessments about young players after only a few games. For instance, when rookie Erling Haaland made an impressive debut for Borussia Dortmund, fans quickly heralded him as a future star, an assumption that has since proven accurate, but was initially based on limited evidence. The opposite can happen as well, where a highly anticipated player may struggle in early games, leading fans to dismiss their potential prematurely.

The JTC bias isn't confined to players alone as it influences how fans perceive coaches, referees, and even entire seasons. In the NFL, a coach might be celebrated as a genius after a few successful games but may quickly find themselves facing criticisms after a short losing streak. A similar trend occurs in European football, where managers of high-profile teams like Real Madrid are under immense pressure to deliver instant results, with fan reactions oscillating wildly between praise and critique. The tendency to jump to conclusions can create a rollercoaster of emotional highs and lows for fans, as each game feels like a defining moment, even if it's only one chapter in a long season.

IMPACT BIAS

Fans tend to overestimate the emotional impact of sports events, also known as 'impact bias', causing them to believe that a game's outcome – whether a victory or a loss – will affect their happiness more than it does. While fans anticipate feeling devastated after a loss or euphoric after a win, the actual emotional impact often fades more quickly than expected. The phenomenon is widespread in sports, as fans build up emotional expectations only to find that the long-term impact is less dramatic than anticipated. One classic example is the FIFA World Cup, where fans can invest months, if not years, into preparing for their country's campaign, expecting it to either make or break their year. In the 2018 World Cup, Germany's early exit shocked and disappointed fans, who had been bracing for a potential repeat of their 2014 championship win. Yet, within weeks, the disappointment faded, with fans shifting their focus to upcoming tournaments and club prospects. Impact bias illustrates how sports, while emotionally intense, produce effects that are more short-lived than fans predict.

Impact bias is also seen in the realization of long-awaited championships. After the Cleveland Cavaliers won their first NBA title in 2016, fans celebrated with exuberance, believing that their city's decades-long championship curse had been broken for good. However, as time passed, fans adjusted to the victory and began looking toward the future, recognizing that the emotional high, while intense, was temporary. Overestimating the long-term emotional effects of sports outcomes reflects a fundamental aspect of fan psychology. Fans tend to anticipate that major events will have lasting consequences even though fans readily adapt to disappointment.

CONFIRMATION BIAS

Confirmation bias, or the tendency to seek out and interpret information that confirms fans' pre-existing beliefs, is a powerful influence in sports fandom, and one that I introduced early in the book. Fans comprehend events, statistics, and outcomes in a way that reinforces their loyalty or justifies their opinions about teams and players. This bias is prominent in regional rivalries. Fans of rival college (American) football teams in the United States, such as Alabama and Auburn, view each other through longstanding preconceptions, interpreting any victory as proof of their team's superiority while minimizing the significance of losses.[9] Even when statistics or external opinions challenge their view, confirmation bias encourages fans to hold onto their beliefs, reinforcing loyalty and intensifying rivalries. In women's sports, confirmation bias comes into play when fans compare female athletes to their male counterparts. Fans sometimes either downplay or overemphasize achievements in women's sports based on stereotyped beliefs about athleticism and competition. For example, fans who believe that women's football lacks the same level of intensity might overlook impressive achievements by players like Marta. On the other hand, fans who are invested in women's sports may highlight the skill and dedication of these players, underscoring the growth of the sport despite fewer resources and historical biases.

SUNK COST FALLACY

The 'sunk cost fallacy' is a bias that occurs when fans continue investing in sporting commitments and allegiances because of the time, money, or energy they've already spent, even if the outcomes are uncertain or disheartening. In sports fandom, the sunk cost fallacy keeps fans loyal to teams through losing seasons, as they feel compelled to continue their support due to years of emotional and financial investment. Fans of long-suffering teams, like the Detroit Lions in the NFL or the Chicago Cubs before their 2016 World Series win, persist in their loyalty. They feel that abandoning their team now would mean all their years of dedication would be wasted. Sunk cost loyalty extends to individual players as well. Tennis fans of players like Andy Murray or Venus Williams continued to support them through injuries or declines in performance, remembering the countless hours they had invested in following their careers. Fans justify their continued support by framing it as loyalty, even when it might make more sense to focus on new or rising players. The sunk cost fallacy is a form of cognitive dissonance that helps fans resolve the conflict between logic and emotion, enabling them to remain devoted despite poor performances or unlikely prospects of success.

One of the reasons fan biases remain so powerful is that fans invest considerable time, money, and emotional energy into their favorite teams and athletes. An investment effect reinforces loyalty, making fans more likely to overlook flaws or justify poor performances because they have already committed so much. Investment biases feature strongly in leagues with high ticket prices, merchandise sales, and travel costs, as fans feel that their financial and emotional contributions make their loyalty more meaningful. In the United States, fans of the NFL's Green Bay Packers display extraordinary dedication to the team, partially because they are not just fans but also shareholders in the franchise. The Packers are unique in the league because they are publicly owned, with fans holding shares in the team. A financial stake creates an added layer of loyalty, as fans view their support as part of a larger community investment. Mixing the emotional and financial attachment leads fans to justify nearly any team decision, as they feel personally connected to the Packers' legacy and success.

MEDIUM MAXIMIZATION

Another concept that sheds light on emotions in fan psychology is 'medium maximization', where fans prioritize measures of prestige, status, or symbolism rather than focusing on results. For example, some fans follow high-status teams, leagues, or players as a way of aligning themselves with symbols of success. By supporting a team like Real Madrid or the Los Angeles Lakers, fans feel that they are part of an elite group, identifying with a brand that symbolizes global influence and historical success. Medium maximization can encourage fans to celebrate individual achievements, such as awards or records as markers of success, even when team performance may be poor. For example, fans of LeBron James closely follow his career milestones, such as his record-breaking points tally or his MVP awards, viewing these achievements as part of his legacy regardless of team performance. A focus on status markers creates a form of vicarious prestige, where fans feel a personal sense of accomplishment in following a successful or famous athlete. The bias isn't limited to mainstream sports. In niche sports like alpine skiing, where athletes like Mikaela Shiffrin have set new records, fans find pride not only in her wins but also in her symbolic achievements. The prestige of breaking records or achieving historical firsts in any sport resonates with fans who view these achievements as reflections of their favorite athlete's significance in the broader landscape of sports.

ATTENTIONAL BIAS

Attentional bias refers to fans' tendency to focus more on certain details while ignoring others, especially when these details align with their expectations or emotions. In sports, attentional bias shapes how fans experience games, directing them to pay more attention to events

that confirm their existing beliefs or support their emotional investment. Often seen in high-stakes games, fans concentrate intensely on
each play, responding to the action in ways that amplify their hopes
or anxieties. One manifestation of attentional bias can be seen in the
rituals fans create around game-watching. Fans of some rugby teams
in South Africa, for example, have a specific routine they follow before
each game, such as gathering with friends, wearing team colors, or
performing a pre-game chant. These rituals become a focal point
for attention, giving fans a sense of control and helping them feel
more engaged in the game. By focusing on pre-game rituals, fans can
channel their energy and attention, reinforcing their commitment
and heightening their emotional experience.

Attentional bias plays a role in how fans assign meaning to signals
of an athlete's performance. In figure skating, for instance, fans who
closely follow a skater like Yuzuru Hanyu might notice subtle aspects
of his routines, such as his footwork or jumps, and conclude they are
indicators of his focus and skill. By zeroing in on these details, fans
form strong opinions based on specific elements of a performance,
often using the observations to reinforce admiration or expectations.
However, attentional bias can also lead fans to overlook unfavorable
elements. For example, fans of Australian Rules football might focus
on their team's aggressive playstyle while disregarding infringements
or rough tactics, viewing these actions through a positive lens.

SOCIAL INFLUENCES AND PUBLIC SIGNALING

Another significant factor in sports fandom is the role of public signaling, where fans express their support openly to gain social recognition or status within their community. The need for social validation
influences fan behavior, making them more likely to invest in costly
displays of loyalty like attending games and purchasing expensive
merchandise. Signaling typically accompanies intense sports rivalries where fan identity becomes a public declaration of allegiance.
For example, in the longstanding MLB rivalry between the Boston
Red Sox and the New York Yankees, fans of both teams take pride

in showing off their team loyalty through hats, jerseys, and public displays of support. By wearing their team's colors or attending games, fans signal their commitment to their chosen side, establishing a sense of identity that sets them apart from rival fans. Social signaling encourages fans to stay loyal and even exaggerate their allegiance, as they want to be seen as authentic and even as 'hardcore' fans by their peers. In cricket, fans of the Indian Premier League (IPL) teams, such as the Mumbai Indians or Chennai Super Kings, engage in public signaling by joining fan clubs, attending matches in team colors, and sharing their support on social media.

Signaling can cascade into rituals. In German football, fans of Borussia Dortmund perform the traditional 'Yellow Wall', where thousands of supporters stand in coordinated sections, creating an intimidating and visually striking show of support. Similarly, in American college football, fans of the University of Alabama perform the 'Roll Tide' chant, a ritualized cheer that has become synonymous with the team. Rituals can also be deeply personal, like a fan's pre-game routine or lucky charm. In Japan, some baseball fans bring small items or talismans believed to bring luck to their favorite team, adding a personal ritual to the game-watching experience. As I noted earlier, these rituals may not directly impact the game, but they provide fans with a sense of control and comfort, making the experience feel more personally meaningful.

Sports fandom can also be shaped by shared morals and values within fan communities. Fans feel a moral obligation to support their team, adhering to group norms and unwritten rules that define what it means to be a genuine fan. Moral standards influence fan behavior, creating a sense of accountability within the fan base, such as a willingness to support their team through adversity. In English football, fans of clubs like Sunderland or Portsmouth can feel a strong moral duty to stick with their team, even when they face relegation or financial struggles. A commitment to stick by the team reflects an ethical stance, where loyalty is seen as a virtue, and abandoning the team is viewed as a betrayal.

FEELING THE THINKING

The psychological principles behind sports fandom show us that being a fan is more than a hobby; it's an integral part of a person's identity, shaped by deep cognitive and emotional processes that shape fans' behaviors and tie them to their teams and communities. Fans often define themselves through their support for a team, which becomes a part of who they are and how they interact with the world around them. Identity formation is reinforced through cognitive biases, emotional investments, rituals, and the implicit values associated with public fandom. In sports like hockey, die-hard fans of NHL teams like the Montreal Canadiens or the Toronto Maple Leafs refer to themselves as 'Habs' or 'Leafs' fans with a level of pride that's like a national identity. Attachment to the team goes beyond individual players or game outcomes and becomes a cultural identity that fans carry with them in every aspect of life. When the Canadiens or Maple Leafs perform well, fans feel validated and uplifted. When they struggle, fans often take it as a personal misfortune.

The fusion of identity and fandom reflects a cognitive phenomenon where sports beliefs function as a core part of self-identity, mediated by potent emotional reinforcement. For example, an intractable sense of identity is evident in rugby fans of the South African Springboks. For many South Africans, the Springboks symbolize resilience, pride, and national unity, particularly after the team's victory in the 1995 Rugby World Cup, which helped bridge racial divides in post-apartheid South Africa. In basketball, fans of the Los Angeles Lakers identify with the team's 'showtime' legacy, and the glamour associated with its history. For these fans, supporting the Lakers is also about belonging to a community that values excellence, style, and entertainment. The team's success over decades has built a fan culture that goes beyond the game, influencing fashion, language, and even lifestyle choices.

My exploration of the sports fan psychology can be summarized in seven key propositions that help explain why our minds are so receptive to sports beliefs and why fandom becomes a significant and emotional part of fans' lives.

PROPOSITION 1: SPORTS PROVIDE NATURAL COGNITIVE CONTENT

Sports thoughts and beliefs occur naturally in the mind, just as thoughts about family, work, or social connections do. The cognitive processes fans use to understand people, roles, and interactions in other parts of life easily apply to sports. For instance, a fan watching their team strategize and execute plays uses the same cognitive skills as they would to observe and interpret social dynamics in everyday life.[10]

PROPOSITION 2: SPORTS CONTENT IS MEMORABLE

Sports beliefs are memorable because they often contain counter-intuitive elements like unexpected twists, remarkable feats, and dramatic failures that go against expectations.[11] These elements capture fans' attention and enhance recall, making sports events easier to remember. When an athlete like Usain Bolt shatters a world record, or when Simone Biles performs gravity-defying routines, fans are more likely to remember these moments because they challenge conventional understandings of human limitations.

PROPOSITION 3: SPORTS DELIVER MEANINGFUL EXPERIENCES

The mind's natural tendency to seek meaning transforms sports into a powerful source of purpose and fulfillment. Fans assign personal significance to their team's victories and losses, viewing them as part of a larger narrative that resonates with their own experiences.[12] For example, when Leicester City won the Premier League in 2016, fans saw it as a 'David vs. Goliath' story, finding inspiration in the team's triumph as an underdog.

PROPOSITION 4: SPORTS ENCOURAGE SHARED INTENTIONS

Sports fandom is strengthened by fans' ability to infer the intentions of others. Fans naturally assume that their fellow supporters share similar hopes, values, and expectations. A shared understanding creates a sense of unity, as fans collectively experience the highs and lows of a season.[13] When a team like Liverpool FC clinches a comeback victory, fans worldwide feel a shared thrill, knowing that millions of others are celebrating alongside them.

PROPOSITION 5: SPORTS GENERATE EMOTIONAL ENGAGEMENT AND EMPATHY

Fans' capacity to detect and empathize with emotions enhances the sports experience, allowing them to connect deeply with the players' struggles, victories, and defeats.[14] Empathy fosters a powerful emotional bond, as fans feel each play, goal, or point as though it were their own. When Tiger Woods completed his comeback win at the 2019 Masters, fans felt his emotional journey, reliving years of resilience and dedication through his success.

PROPOSITION 6: SPORTS DISPLAY COMMITMENT THROUGH COSTLY SIGNALS

The mind's inclination toward social exchange encourages fans to make costly commitments to their teams, whether through time, money, or emotional investment. These sacrifices signal dedication and reinforce social bonds, as fans show that they value their team and fellow fans over individual gain.[15] For instance, fans who travel long distances or buy season tickets despite economic limitations demonstrate their commitment, creating a sense of authenticity and belonging within the fan community.

PROPOSITION 7: SPORTS CREATE GROUP MORALITY

The mind's innate moral intuition strengthens fan communities, as fans adopt a shared sense of right and wrong within the context of their sport. These morals define what it means to be a true fan, shaping interactions within the community and establishing behavioral norms. But that doesn't mean that fans are exemplars of ethical virtue. For many player, athlete, club, team, and national loyalists, being a true fan means celebrating the losses and failures of adversaries as vigorously as their own triumphs.[16]

CONCLUSION: THE COGNITIVE-EMOTIONAL FOUNDATIONS OF SPORTS FANDOM

The mind's cognitive structure – designed to connect, empathize, remember, and find meaning – makes it naturally receptive to sports beliefs imbued with emotional resonance. Mental architecture explains why sports fandom is so powerful, uniting people across cultures, generations, and backgrounds. Through cognitive and emotional processes, sports become more than just games; they become rituals of identity, expressions of loyalty, and sources of shared purpose. The seven propositions illuminate the psychology behind fandom, showing us that sports fandom is more than just an interest or pastime. It is an extension of natural human tendencies. By attributing meaning to team successes, and forming moral codes within fan communities, sports fandom fulfills deep psychological needs for connection, significance, and self-expression. In the end, sports tap into some of the oldest and most universal aspects of human nature. Whether it's the emotional thrill of watching a last-minute goal or the quiet pride in wearing a team jersey, sports fandom reflects the human desire to belong, to believe, and to be part of something greater. The psychology of sports fandom reveals how minds are uniquely structured to find meaning and connection through the teams, players, and events that captivate fans' hearts and minds. In the following chapter I show how extreme fandom can even match levels of religious devotion.

NOTES

1 Schachter, S., & Singer, J. E. (2021). Cognitive appraisal and emotional arousal in sports. *Cognition and Emotion*, 35(2), 112–130.

2 Lazarus, R. S. (2020). Emotion and adaptation in sports. *Journal of Sport and Exercise Psychology*, 42(1), 15–29.

3 Zillmann, D., Bryant, J., & Sapolsky, B. S. (2021). Excitation transfer in sports fans: Why emotions linger after games. *Media Psychology*, 24(2), 178–194.

4 Gantz, W., & Lewis, N. (2021). Sports fandom and mood regulation: How watching games affects emotional well-being. *Communication and Sport*, 9(3), 411–429.

5 Friesen, A. P., Lane, A. M., Devonport, T. J., & Stanley, D. M. (2021). Emotional intelligence and sports fan behavior. *International Journal of Sport Psychology*, 52(4), 289–308.

6 Ramanayaka, N. D., Dickson, G., & Rayne, D. (2024). Heuristics in sport: A scoping review. *Psychology of Sport and Exercise*, 71, 102589.

7 Hastorf, A. H., & Cantril, H. (2020). They saw a game: A case study in biased perception. *Journal of Experimental Social Psychology*, 82, 124–139.

8 Plessner, H., & Haar, T. (2006). Sports performance judgments from a social cognitive perspective. *Psychology of Sport and Exercise*, 7(6), 555–575.

9 Gross, J. J. (2019). The role of emotion regulation in sports fandom. *Emotion Review*, 11(3), 207–219.

10 Ekkekakis, P., & Brand, R. (2020). Affective responses to sports competition: The psychology of wins and losses. *Psychology of Sport and Exercise*, 46, 101577.

11 LeDoux, J. E. (2021). Emotional memory and sports fandom: How the brain remembers significant moments. *Neuroscience and Biobehavioral Reviews*, 125, 365–378.

12 David, P., Horton, B., & German, C. (2022). The impact of nostalgia in sports fandom: Memory, emotions, and attachment. *Sport in Society*, 25(6), 847–864.

13 Rimé, B. (2020). Social sharing of emotions in sports: Why fans seek collective experiences. *Emotion*, 20(4), 523–539.

14 Ochsner, K. N., & Gross, J. J. (2019). The neural basis of emotion and cognitive control in sports spectatorship. *Annual Review of Psychology*, 70, 739–766.

15 Tamir, M., & Ford, B. Q. (2019). When wanting to feel bad is good: Emotion regulation in sports spectatorship. *Journal of Personality and Social Psychology*, 116(3), 560–578.

16 Vallerand, R. J., Ntoumanis, N., & Philippe, F. L. (2021). The dualistic model of passion in sports fandom. *Motivation and Emotion*, 45(2), 113–129.

4

THE PSYCHOLOGY OF SPORTS MEANING

INTRODUCTION: WHY SPORTS MATTER

This book is all about why, for billions around the world, sports fandom is an essential part of life that stirs the soul, sparks intense loyalty, and even sometimes pushes fans over the limit. As the previous chapter emphasized, this intense emotional reaction speaks to how deeply fans connect with their favorite teams and players or athletes. The question this chapter considers is whether the impact of sports fandom goes beyond mere enjoyment or heartbreak: could sports hold a similar place in fans' lives as religion, providing a source of existential meaning? Many fans and commentators have observed that sports, like religion, elicit deep emotional reactions that include goosebumps, tears, and euphoria. My proposition is that by exploring how the brain processes these experiences, we can get a better understanding of why sports become so deeply embedded in fans' lives. By describing what happens in the brain during fandom, this chapter aims to explain why sports resonate so powerfully and why, for many, they're nothing short of sacred.

In this chapter I build on the previous one by further detailing how sport fandom taps into deep emotions, rituals, and even spiritual experiences that connect fans to something larger than themselves. It

DOI: 10.4324/9781003587699-4

uncovers the ways in which sports fandom can mirror religious devotion, examining the brain's response to intense moments, the symbolic power of team loyalty, and the rituals that transform ordinary spectators into dedicated communities. I also consider the psychological impact of collective experiences, showing how shared chants, synchronized movements, and symbols not only create unity, but also bring about powerful, almost mystical, states of mind.

SPIRITUAL BRAINS AND SACRED SPORTS

When we think about the sacred or the spiritual, most people imagine religious rituals or meditative practices. But neuroscience is beginning to show that certain kinds of intense experiences may stimulate the brain just like spiritual experiences.[1] For example, spiritual experiences are associated with a unique brain state involving the limbic system, an old part of the brain, and an area associated with emotion and memory. Unsurprisingly, these same regions are also heavily activated during key sports experiences, which might explain why fans feel moments of profound connection with their teams. Here I consider what happens inside the brain when fans experience peak moments during sports fandom. The goal is to investigate how sports can generate such strong emotions and create life-altering meaning, driven by powerful brain mechanisms that underpin team loyalty.

Let's start with the idea that perhaps spiritual experiences don't always have to be religious. In fact, powerful experiences can come from sports events that profoundly impact fans. The connection between spirituality and sports may seem speculative, but it's becoming more accepted as we learn more about the brain.[2] Emotions are governed by both the ancient, primal parts of the brain, such as the limbic system, and the more thoughtful, reasoning regions, like the frontal cortex. It's in this blend of ancient brain functions and modern thinking that we find the key to understanding why sports affect fans so significantly.[3] Brain scans have shown that certain peak experiences, such as those associated with religious rituals, sports victories, or high-stakes competition, can activate this interplay between emotional and rational brain regions.[4] Consider, for example, the widespread national fervor around events like the Olympic Games. Watching Simone Biles defy gravity in gymnastics or cricket star Virat Kohli hit a sublime match-winning run can create an almost trance-like state for spectators.[5] Critical moments in sport are captivating not only for their physical skill but also for the way they tap into something mysterious that holds fans in awe and makes them feel a part of something transcendent. It turns out that the mechanisms driving the response are embedded in the brain's wiring and chemistry.

HOW THE BRAIN BONDS FANS

In some cases, fans bond more strongly with their teams when they've been through tough times together. People tend to form tight-knit groups when facing challenges, a phenomenon seen not only in sports but in many areas of life, from military training to intense office team projects. Such bonding is known as 'identity fusion' and happens when people's personal and group identities become so intertwined that they start to see the team's identity as part of their own.[6] For example, the fans of Brazilian football club Palmeiras are known for their loyalty, especially when the team has faced struggles. Palmeiras fans often refer to themselves as part of the 'Palmeirense Family', reflecting the deep, familial connection they feel to the team. Intense bonding leads to elaborate displays of devotion, including choreographed songs, flags, and marches that bring the community together and reaffirm their shared identity.

There's more to these fan experiences than meets the eye. Scientists have observed that, on a neurological level, fans experience a kind of non-romantic love for their teams that activates the same brain regions involved in other close bonds. Research has also found that fans' stress hormone levels – specifically cortisol – increase significantly during high-stakes matches.[7] Notably, the highest cortisol spikes are recorded in fans who report the strongest sense of identification with their team. Other research has used what is called neuroimaging (fMRI) scans to take pictures of fans' brain activity as they watch their team win or lose.[8] Fans of English Premier League teams show heightened brain activity in the amygdala, an area tied to emotion, as well as in reward-related areas of the brain. Fandom appears to activate the same pathways in the brain as strong personal relationships, making team loyalty a genuine emotional attachment that goes beyond a casual interest in the game. If you are interested in more details on these studies and the inner workings of the brain you can find some excellent resources in the recommended reading section at the end of this book.

The bonding effects seen in fan groups can also lead to more extreme behaviors.[9] For instance, when fans of competing teams clash at a match, their brains are reacting with a 'fight or flight' response triggered by the perceived threat of the rival group. Examples of similar psychological intensity can even be seen among fans of smaller, less publicized sports. Take, for instance, wrestling fans in Mongolia, where the national sport, 'Bökh', holds deep cultural significance. Here, fans come together in large numbers to support their local wrestlers, cheering and celebrating with unique ceremonial songs and dances. Even in moments of loss, the emotional attachment doesn't fade. In fact, it often strengthens as fans bond over shared loyalty to a proud tradition.

Studies on social identity suggest that the strong identification with a sports team can amplify feelings of 'us versus them'. While this can foster camaraderie within a fan group, it can also create tension with opposing groups. Consider the fierce rivalry I've mentioned several times between Celtic FC and Rangers FC in Scotland. Based in long historical and religious differences, the enmity occasionally spills over into aggression. Although most fans support their teams peacefully, the tribal loyalty felt by some can lead to instances of hostility and conflict.

On a more positive note, however, strong fan identities also foster inclusivity and community support. Many teams use their influence to bring people together for positive causes, creating bonds that extend beyond the sport itself. For instance, fans of the Egyptian team Al Ahly regularly organize community events and charity drives, leveraging their group loyalty for social impact. The loyalty and solidarity within fan groups highlight how sports can cultivate belonging with a sense of social responsibility and purpose.

LOSING YOURSELF IN THE GAME

For some fans, sports provide a rare chance to experience 'flow', a state where time seems to vanish, replaced by a feeling of being totally absorbed in the moment. The flow mental state, often described as 'being in the zone', occurs when there's a perfect balance between challenge and skill.[10] Flow states are common for athletes, but they're not limited to players alone. Fans can enter a flow state while watching a game in a packed stadium, surrounded by others who are equally absorbed.

Studies have shown that live sports offer a far better chance of reaching a flow state than watching from home, as the shared energy in the stadium helps fans immerse themselves completely in the experience. Being at a live event often means not only watching the game but also participating in group chants, movements, and cheers. Group actions heighten the sense of connection and increase the likelihood of reaching that immersive flow state. For example, in Argentina, fans of football club Boca Juniors gather in huge crowds to perform the 'la 12' cheer, a coordinated group chant and movement. Similarly, fans of the Turkish football team Galatasaray are famous for their 'Hell of Galatasaray' chant, creating an intimidating atmosphere for visiting teams.

When in a flow state, fans seamlessly shift their attention from one aspect of the game to another without getting distracted, experiencing a heightened sense of satisfaction and even euphoria. Rapid attentional shifting, as psychologists call it, is a common feature of flow states and is linked to feelings of joy and fulfillment. Dopamine, a brain chemical that influences motivation and pleasure, plays a central role in sustaining flow states. When fans focus intensely on a game or a ritual, dopamine levels increase, helping fans tune in to the game and shut out distractions. The release of dopamine enhances enjoyment of the experience, making it even more satisfying.[11] Its presence further explains why fans report a sense of elation during intense games, especially when they feel deeply connected to the team and the surrounding fans. Imagine a packed stadium during a nail-biting final like the Indian Premier League (IPL) cricket finals or a Copa Libertadores football match in South America. The fans' chants and claps create a hypnotic atmosphere. Their synchronized actions, movements, and collective cheering pull each person into a focused, shared mental state, making the entire crowd feel unified.[12] The neurochemicals triggered by these collective experiences amplify the connection between fans and intensify their feelings of loyalty, purpose, and enjoyment.

Dopamine-driven pleasure is part of what makes sports fandom somewhat addictive. For instance, fans of cricket in India or of Australian rules football experience a natural high during moments of suspense or last-minute victory, reinforcing their desire to repeat the experience. It is especially true during events with cultural or symbolic weight, such as India's cricket matches against Pakistan or the Australian Football League Grand Final. Fans look forward to these events with tremendous anticipation, and the dopamine spikes during peak moments of the game intensify their enjoyment, solidifying their loyalty.

Even the ritualistic aspects of fandom, like singing the team anthem or performing a specific cheer, can stimulate dopamine production, as the brain associates these actions with positive feelings. For example, rugby fans in Wales singing their anthem, 'Hen Wlad Fy Nhadau' ('Land of My Fathers'), report feelings of unity, pride, and even joy as their voices fill the stadium. Combined with the emotional context of the match, the ritual elevates dopamine levels, making the experience both memorable and resonant.

Not only do fans share physical behaviors, but they can also synchronize their emotions with the players they are observing, as well as other spectators. The phenomenon is known as 'emotional contagion', where observing others' emotions can trigger similar feelings in the watcher. As a result, fans can experience a wave of joy or despair together, reacting to the highs and lows of the game as one emotional unit. When fans see their favorite player succeed or struggle, their brains activate areas linked to empathy and shared experience, mirroring the players' emotional states.

Consider the emotional impact of watching a star player, like Japan's Naomi Osaka during a Grand Slam tennis match, overcoming a tough opponent. The tension and focus on her face, as well as the energy in her movements, can affect her fans in a way that almost makes them feel as though they are playing right alongside her. Shared empathy strengthens fan–player bonds and creates what is called 'vicarious agency' where fans experience a sense of involvement in, or influence over, the game's outcome. For example, fans display 'body English', an unconscious imitation of a player's movements, particularly in high-stakes situations. When a fan sees Brazilian football sensation Marta making an agile move toward the goal, they might instinctively lean forward or clench their fists as if they're participating in her skillful play. The mirroring reaction extends the emotional bond, pulling fans further into the experience and creating the sense of unity fans feel with certain players or athletes.

The emotions that fans experience are both personal and collective, as fans absorb the feelings of those around them.[13] Watching a sporting event with a large crowd creates an environment where emotions flow between individuals, amplifying the impact of each reaction. Studies have found that shared emotional reactions in groups can stimulate the release of oxytocin, a hormone associated with bonding and social connection. The release of oxytocin may help explain why fans feel such strong tribal bonding with each other during high-stakes matches. When fans experience joy or sadness together, the resulting oxytocin surge strengthens their social ties, creating a sense of unity that can last beyond the match itself.

The visual and physical intensity of sports is another element that triggers powerful reactions in the brain. Observing the smooth athleticism of Kenyan marathon runner Eliud Kipchoge or the swift agility of New Zealand rugby player Portia Woodman stimulates areas of the brain associated with admiration and motivation. Psychologists suggest that witnessing such peak physical performances encourages a kind of 'motor resonance', where the viewer's brain mirrors the physical movements and emotions of the athlete. The mirror effect is not exclusive to elite sports and can occur anytime a fan observes an impressive physical display. For example, many South African fans watching Wayde van Niekerk break the 400m world record in track experienced a collective sense of awe and excitement. Engagement is not just emotional but neurological, involving specific brain regions that help fans feel connected to the performance on a deeper level. Some sporting performances are so remarkable that any observer will likely feel something.

Watching sports can even activate areas of the brain that engage when viewing other stimulating imagery, such as art or dance. The aesthetics of sports, from the grace of figure skating to the strength of weightlifting, provide fans with a captivating visual target, creating conditions that allow for transformative experiences. Fans find themselves entranced by the athletes' movements, feeling inspired and connected to the essence of the performance, much like an audience might be moved by a powerful ballet or opera.

THE ROLE OF RITUALS IN MEANING

As I mentioned several times in earlier chapters, rituals play a big part in connecting fans to their teams. Just as religious practices often involve elaborate routines that signal commitment, sports fans engage in their own pre-game and post-game rituals that create a sense of belonging and meaning. Rituals can range from simple actions, like wearing a lucky jersey, to more complex sequences, like the fan traditions seen at FC Barcelona's home stadium, where fans display a large mosaic using colored cards before every match.

Some rituals can be highly professional, like those practiced by fans of the South Korean baseball team the LG Twins, who perform a specific dance with a handkerchief whenever the team scores. Other rituals have historical roots, such as the tradition of baseball fans in the United States singing 'Take Me Out to the Ball Game' during the seventh inning stretch. Though unique to different sports and cultures, rituals create routines that makes fans feel part of a larger community. Another compelling example of a fan ritual comes from Iceland, where fans perform the 'Viking Clap' in unison, each clap interspaced with a thunderous 'huh' chant. A simple yet powerful gesture, the clap unites Icelandic football fans and players in a way that simultaneously bonds practitioners and intimidates rivals. It's memorable for fans while further intensifying their sense of connection and pride, reinforcing the meaning behind each match one clap at a time.

The psychological power of sports rituals lies in their repetition and structure, which cultivates consistency and predictability. Rituals embed in fans' minds as symbols of unity and loyalty that need no explanation. Fans rarely ask themselves why they're performing these routines; they just know they feel right. Much like religious rituals, sports rituals become ingrained, automatic actions that provide comfort and fortify identity. A traditional example is seen in the Australian Football League, where fans working for teams create large, handmade banners for the players to run through at the start of each match. The banners require hours of preparation by fan volunteers, who build custom banners with bespoke messages and designs every game, only to have them torn apart in moments as the players run through them. For fans, the banner represents a unique, team-specific tradition. It ties them to the players and gives them a feeling of contribution, even though each banner is always destroyed.

Fans also carry out traditions that have little practical purpose beyond emotional or symbolic significance. For instance, supporters of Japan's Yokohama F. Marinos football club participate in an elaborate pre-game ritual where they wave large, hand-painted flags, creating a visually stunning display that fosters a sense of collective pride and participation. While these actions may not directly impact the game's outcome, they reinforce bonds within the fan community, making them feel like they're part of a greater purpose.

While team rituals are widely shared, individual fans often personalize their own game-day routines. Fans' unique actions might look quirky or even irrational from the outside, but they carry profound meaning for the individual. In Argentina, for example, a well-known football fan tradition involves fans holding onto 'lucky' items like scarves or jerseys for years – sometimes without washing them – believing that these objects can influence the game. Fans of Boca Juniors, for example, have been known to carry their jerseys and scarves to every game, convinced that the items bring luck to the players. Similarly, some fans create personalized superstitions or small rituals intended to bring fortune to their teams. In Turkey, supporters of football club Fenerbahçe carry out their own special acts at home games, such as tapping their seats in a specific pattern or standing up at precise moments, believing that these actions contribute to their team's success. Although personal routines may seem trivial, they provide a sense of control and reinforce personal connection to the sport. It creates a unique sense of belonging that strengthens each time the fan performs their ritual. Fans of some teams go even further, creating organized displays of loyalty and devotion. The fans of South Korea's FC Seoul, known for their meticulously coordinated displays, perform a synchronized cheer, moving in unison to create a visual and emotional spectacle. These displays of unity foster an even stronger sense of togetherness and identity, showing how fan rituals can go from the individual to the collective, creating an experience that feels sacred.

SYMBOLS AND IMAGERY

Brains are hardwired to respond to symbols, from national flags to team colors. Some of these symbols, like the fierce animal mascots in rugby or football, evoke primal instincts. When images are coupled with powerful music or chants, they magnify the tribal experience that many sports fans crave. Just as in religious ceremonies where symbols and rituals carry deep meaning, sports teams use logos, mascots, colors, and songs to create a shared identity. Sports fans therefore employ symbols to heighten the emotional impact of their rituals, and might include face paint, costumes, flags, and chants, which act as visual markers of loyalty that help create a shared language among fans. The colors of a team jersey or a certain chant carry emotional significance that is understood immediately by fans, even without spoken words. For example, supporters of Al Ahly SC, one of the biggest football clubs in Egypt, wear their team's iconic red and white colors as a show of unity, while collectively chanting songs that have been passed down for generations. In South Africa, fans of the Springboks rugby team have their own symbolic gestures, wearing green and gold with pride and creating displays that reflect the team's historical significance. Colors represent not only the team but also a sense of national pride, with the emblematic springbok, an agile antelope native to the region, acting as a poignant cultural and emotional symbol. Symbols like these help fans create a mental and emotional association with the team, reinforcing a shared identity.

Symbols in sports fandom function similarly to religious icons. Just as a cross might signify devotion in certain religions, the emblems and colors of sports teams evoke loyalty and belonging. Symbols serve as cognitive shortcuts that instantly trigger a fan's emotional memory, recalling past games, victories, and even painful losses. Symbols are essential for both individual fans and fan communities, as they encapsulate the spirit of the team in a single, recognizable image.

For young fans, the symbolism and rituals associated with their favorite team are often introduced by family members, friends, or other fans. The practice creates an unbroken historical chain of cultural inheritance. Adolescence is a critical period for developing lifelong attachments, as the brain is especially receptive to forming strong associations and creating emotional memories. For instance, many football fans in Brazil inherit their love for the sport and a specific team, like Flamengo or Santos, from their parents or grandparents, who take them to games from a young age, creating a tradition that binds the family across generations.

Similar generational bequeathing of fandom is seen among cricket fans in Pakistan and India, where children learn the rules, chants, and even local cricket folklore from older relatives. Cricket holds a special cultural status in these countries, where matches are community events. In Pakistan, young fans cheer for the national team alongside family members, waving the green and white Pakistani flag, bonding over the shared pride of representing their country on the global stage. Generational rituals are marked by special family traditions, such as gathering to watch games on television or traveling together to support the team in nearby towns. Young fans who engage in these routines are more likely to become lifelong fans. They absorb the emotional and symbolic aspects of their family's fandom, strengthening their identification with the team.

RITUALS OF INCLUSION

Fan rituals drive social bonding, helping to integrate fans into a community and make them feel like valued members. Fan groups develop unique customs and behaviors that solidify the connection between members. For example, 'The Kop', Liverpool FC's iconic fan group, is known for its powerful anthem, 'You'll Never Walk Alone', which fans sing in unison before every home game. Similarly, fans of the Blue Bulls rugby team in South Africa perform elaborate rituals that include wearing the team's distinctive blue jersey, chanting team anthems, and waving blue flags. Some fan rituals develop spontaneously and assume greater meaning as they become part of the team's culture. For instance, Kaizer Chiefs fans in South Africa have a vibrant and dedicated group known as the 'Amakhosi for Life', which organizes and leads coordinated cheers and dances in the stands. The Amakhosi group's enthusiastic rituals add to the experience of watching a Chiefs game, a bit like the English cricket fan group, the 'Barmy Army'.

To an outsider, some fan rituals might appear strange, even 'crazy', but these behaviors play an important role in building trust within the group. Performing seemingly irrational actions can reinforce trust and authenticity among fans because they demand a personal sacrifice, proving the fan's commitment to the group. It explains why fans of certain teams wear specific colors or outfits, even in extreme weather, or why some spend hours creating intricate banners and flags. Fans are more likely to trust others who perform similar rituals, even if those actions seem unusual. Shared rituals signal a fan's commitment to the group, making them a reliable ally. For example, fans of Morocco's Raja Casablanca football team are known for their visually stunning 'tifo' displays, where thousands of fans work together to create huge, colorful images in the stands. Not only do the displays showcase fan creativity but they also send a message of unity and commitment to each other and to their team. Unusual rituals serve as a kind of 'badge' for fans, signaling their authenticity to others in the group. By participating in these unconventional activities, fans show that they're not casual spectators but dedicated supporters willing to invest their time and energy for the team. A shared commitment helps build stronger, more resilient fan communities where each member feels validated and accepted.

When fans engage in symbolic rituals they're also internalizing and expressing cultural values. By performing rituals, fans connect with each other through a shared symbolic language; one that may include visual symbols (team logos and colors), songs, and chants. Symbols become cognitive anchors, tying fans to their team's identity and history, reinforcing both personal and collective meaning. For a fan of the Argentine football team River Plate, the iconic red diagonal stripe across the team's white jersey represents a symbol of the team's legacy and the intense loyalty it commands.

The impact of ritualized symbols isn't limited to national or mainstream sports. For instance, netball fans in New Zealand passionately support their national team, the Silver Ferns, with chants and symbols that include the native silver fern plant. The silver fern represents not just the team but the nation, and the fans' dedication to this emblem deepens their emotional bond with both the team and each other. While the immediate experience of a sports event provides excitement, the rituals associated with fandom can have long-lasting psychological effects. Repeated rituals reinforce loyalty and group identity, creating a sense of fulfillment and belonging that fans carry with them long after the game ends. Psychologists note that repeated engagement with fan rituals can foster a mild addiction where fans return to the game seeking the same emotional high that they've previously experienced.

Over time, the continued engagement with fan rituals and experiences can even create lasting changes in the brain.[14] Strong, emotionally charged memories like those associated with intense sports moments can shape long-term emotional attachments and personal identity. The effect is like how deeply religious or cultural rituals can imprint on people's memories and shape their values and beliefs. One example of this long-lasting impact can be seen in fans of rugby in Fiji, where the sport is a cultural staple. Fijian fans view rugby as a symbol of community and resilience, with traditional songs, dances, and rituals forming part of the fan experience.

There's a connection between rituals, flow states, and symbols that might facilitate the experience of altered states of consciousness. For centuries, spiritual practices have involved repetitive actions like chanting, dancing, or drumming to induce these states. Sports rituals often use similar elements, such as rhythmic clapping, coordinated chants, and emotional songs. Shared actions can shift the brain into a state where fans experience a collective euphoria, blurring the line between the individual and the group. For example, I've mentioned how fans of the German Bundesliga's Borussia Dortmund create a unified chant that resonates through their iconic 'Yellow Wall' section of the stadium. As a synchronized display of thousands of fans clapping and chanting in unison, the spectacle cultivates a sensory environment that heightens the fans' emotional experience. Repetition, combined with the cultural significance of the ritual, may help fans enter a state like that of traditional spiritual practices, where personal identity merges with the group.

Another essential element in sports fandom linked through rituals is music, which has been shown to engage the brain in ways that increase focus, excitement, and emotion. Music can provide a soundtrack that enhances the spectator experience. In sports settings it can deliver auditory cues that activate the brain's emotional centers, adding layers of meaning to the experience. When combined with visual elements like colorful flags, lights, or choreographed displays, music strengthens sensory immersion. Fans of the Colombian football team Atlético Nacional, for instance, participate in vibrant stadium-wide displays of green and white, complemented by loud music and choreographed movements, creating a ritualized sensory environment. The effect of numerous combined sensory cues including symbols, music, color, and sound works in the same way as religious ceremonies to add gravity to significant moments and amplify devotion. When fans repeatedly engage in rituals, they strengthen their emotional attachment to the team, creating a conditioned response where the sights and sounds of the stadium and other fans immediately evoke excitement and loyalty.

CONCLUSION: THE SACRED AND THE STADIUM

This chapter has highlighted the brain's response to peak experiences, the role of ritual in fostering unity, and the ways in which shared symbols and synchronized actions can evoke profound emotions and even altered states of consciousness. Sports fandom, much like religious practice, serves as a grounding force that provides comfort, connection, and purpose. Attachment to a team becomes a journey of shared highs and lows that bonds individuals to one another, creating a unique sense of belonging that transcends the boundaries of the game. This powerful blend of psychology, ritual, and community illustrates why, for billions around the world, sports are not just entertainment, but a quintessential part of the human experience.

By connecting to fans' deepest social instincts and tapping into powerful neurological responses, sports provide them with a sense of purpose and meaning that is both enduring and transformative. The rituals of fandom serve as cognitive anchors, reinforcing the emotional bond between fans and their teams, and creating a shared language that brings people together, often across vast cultural divides. In the end, sports fandom isn't just about watching a game. It's about being part of something larger, feeling a sense of unity with others, and experiencing moments of intense emotion that can be both exhilarating and comforting.[15] For fans around the world, from the rugby fields of Fiji to the football stadiums of Egypt, sports offer a way to celebrate, express identity, and feel connected in a world that can sometimes feel divided. Through rituals, symbols, and shared experiences, fans create a unique kind of community that transcends the game itself and becomes a lasting source of meaning and joy in their lives.[16]

NOTES

1 Anderson, C., & Carnagey, N. L. (2018). Emotional and psychological responses to sports competition: The neuroscience of fandom. *Journal of Sport and Exercise Psychology*, 40(3), 220–235.

2 Stępień, K. B., & Małolepszy, E. (2022). Sports fandom and spirituality: Exploring transcendence through collective experiences. *Journal of Sport and Social Issues*, 46(3), 290–306.

3 Fiske, S. T., & Taylor, S. E. (2013). *Social cognition: From brains to culture*. Sage Publications.

4 Van Cappellen, P., & Rimé, B. (2014). Collective effervescence and shared rituals in sports and religion. *Emotion Review*, 6(4), 268–273.

5 Zillmann, D., & Paulus, P. B. (1993). Spectators: Reactions to sports events and their social consequences. *Journal of Social Issues*, 49(4), 15–34.

6 Newson, M., Buhrmester, M., & Whitehouse, H. (2021). Football, fan violence, and identity fusion. *Current Directions in Psychological Science*, 30(2), 148–154.

7 Newson, M., Shiramizu, V., Buhrmester, M., Hattori, W., Jong, J., Yamamoto, E., & Whitehouse, H. (2020). Devoted fans release more cortisol when watching live soccer matches. *Stress and Health*, 36(2), 220–227.

8 Cayolla, R., Biscaia, R., Baumeister, R. F., Fetscherin, M., Brito-Costa, S., Duarte, I. C., & Castelo-Branco, M. (2024). The neural bases of sport fan reactions to teams: Evidence from a neuroimaging study. *Journal of Consumer Behaviour*, 23(2), 842–854.

9 Deci, E. L., & Ryan, R. M. (2000). The 'what' and 'why' of goal pursuits: Human needs and the self-determination of behavior. *Psychological Inquiry*, 11(4), 227–268.

10 Csikszentmihalyi, M. (1990). *Flow: The psychology of optimal experience*. Harper & Row.

11 Sato, K., Jung, M., & Kim, H. (2018). The role of dopamine in the psychology of sports spectatorship. *Neuropsychologia*, 119, 1–9.

12 Richardson, D. C., & Dale, R. (2005). Synchronization in groups: The neural basis of shared experience in sports fandom. *Trends in Cognitive Sciences*, 9(12), 578–584.

13 Ashforth, B. E., & Schinoff, B. S. (2016). Identity and identification in organizations: An examination of collective fan identity. *Academy of Management Annals*, 10(1), 1–34.

14 Cayolla, R., Biscaia, R., Baumeister, R. F., Chan, H. Y., Duarte, I. C., & Castelo-Branco, M. (2024). Neural correlates of fanhood: The role of fan identity and team brand strength. *Frontiers in Human Neuroscience*, 17, 1235139.

15 Dunbar, R. I. M. (2021). Friendship, bonding, and the role of oxytocin in team sports. *Adaptive Human Behavior and Physiology*, 7(2), 175–190.

16 Balcells, J., & Salas, M. (2020). The social and psychological effects of sports rituals: A case study of soccer fandom. *International Review for the Sociology of Sport*, 55(5), 609–627.

5

THE PSYCHOLOGY
OF SPORTS FANDOM

INTRODUCTION: THE SEEDS OF
SPORTS FANDOM

Sports fandom is grounded in human nature.[1] Minds are naturally drawn to finding meaning and connection, and sports offer a framework through shared beliefs, rituals, and heroes that unite people into tight-knit communities. These elements create a sense of belonging and purpose that resonates deeply with fans. Whether it's the bursting crowds at Buenos Aires' Bombonera stadium during a Boca Juniors match or the electric energy of Kabaddi arenas in India, sports transcend cultural boundaries to forge shared identities. They offer solace in uncertain times and elevate individuals to legendary status, like New Zealand's rugby icon Jonah Lomu or Indian badminton champion P. V. Sindhu.[2] These champions inspire admiration and even devotion through their remarkable and symbolic achievements.

Being part of a sports tribe comes with responsibilities though.[3] Fans are expected to adhere to rituals and codes of behavior that foster unity and discipline. For example, the elaborate ceremonies practiced by Senegalese wrestling fans and the synchronized chants of South Korean baseball enthusiasts illustrate how sports rituals reinforce group cohesion. Shared identity, much like evolutionary

   DOI: 10.4324/9781003587699-5

group survival strategies, strengthens the bonds within the community, making it more resilient against external challenges.[4] Sports fandom thus operates as a powerful source of collective identity and enduring connection.

The emotional and psychological depth of sports fandom stems from the brain's ability to adopt and defend beliefs that simplify life and make it meaningful.[5] The process is amplified by cultural and social influences, as seen in universally celebrated sports moments. For instance, Cathy Freeman's iconic 400m track gold medal win at the Sydney 2000 Olympics united Australia and became a symbol of hope and reconciliation for Indigenous communities. Fans also internalize shared experiences. Consider the euphoric celebrations in Brazil's favelas after a Seleção victory; moments deeply ingrained through cultural traditions and emotional resonance. Similarly, the achievements of Ethiopian long-distance legend Haile Gebrselassie inspire narratives of perseverance and pride, reflecting how stories tied to sports amplify our innate inclinations.

Minds are also predisposed to find patterns and decipher meaning, which further solidifies fans' connection to sports.[6] For example, cricket fans in India might interpret every tactical move as a stroke of genius when their team triumphs. Such cognitive tractability creates fertile ground for sports beliefs to flourish, fostering long-lasting loyalty and engagement. At the heart of sports beliefs lies unwavering faith in teams, players, and outcomes.[7] Faith underpins 'superordinate' beliefs, the fundamental concepts and ideas so deeply held that they transcend logic or scrutiny, operating as convictions that shape the identity of fans and their collective experiences.

Three defining characteristics underpin sports fans' faith-based beliefs. First, they are resistant to verification. When fans of Lionel Messi passionately argue that he is the greatest footballer of all time, their conviction might defy analytical comparison but resonate emotionally. Second, they are memorable due to their counterintuitively poignant elements. Saudi Arabia's unexpected victory over Argentina in the 2022 FIFA World Cup is a prime example of a story that endures because it contradicted all expectations. Finally, they are profoundly emotional, intertwining with fans' personal stories and experiences, as seen when South African fans celebrated the Springboks' Rugby World Cup triumph; a win that symbolized unity and resilience.

The persistence of sports fan faith is universal, shaped by cognitive adaptations that emphasize group cohesion and survival.[8] Across cultures, this is evident in diverse expressions of fandom. Australian AFL supporters exhibit tribal loyalty rivaling that of European football fans, while Japanese baseball enthusiasts showcase meticulous rituals that reinforce their community ties. Shared belief systems offer fans both personal comfort and opportunities for social connection, making sports a global unifier.

Sports fandom provides a mental framework for navigating uncertainty and complexity. By aligning themselves with a team or player, and against others, fans find a source of hope and stability.[9] The predictability and ritual of sports events further enhance psychological reliance. Weekly matches or annual tournaments act as anchors, bringing structure and continuity to fans' lives. Traditions offer a sense of permanence and meaningful connection, alleviating existential uncertainties.

Sports beliefs go beyond escapism; they cultivate hope and optimism and, even sometimes, proactive pessimism.[10] Fans cling to the promise of future success, regardless of current setbacks. The underdog stories of Kenya's rugby sevens team or Fiji's journey to Olympic gold exemplify the power of belief in overcoming adversity. By investing emotionally in their teams, fans create a psychological wedge that holds open the door to optimism and confidence in a better future.

One of the most significant impacts of sports fandom is its ability to forge strong social bonds.[11] These connections cut across social, economic, and cultural divides, uniting people through shared passion and identity. We see it across sports and geographies. For supporters of women's netball in New Zealand or Egypt's Al Ahly football fans, cheering for their team fosters a powerful and defining sense of belonging. Sports fandom also structures social interactions, creating transparent hierarchies and norms. For instance, South Korean esports fans gain recognition within their communities through dedication and knowledge, mirroring the dynamics seen in traditional sports. These networks provide validation as well as opportunities for individuals to find their place within a community.

Ultimately, sports fandom reflects the brain's natural inclination to form belief systems that provide meaning and social purpose. From the thrilling victories of Nigeria's women's football team to the precision of Chinese table tennis champions, sports generate shared narratives that captivate and unite. By embracing these stories, fans accumulate existential capital.[12]

At first glance, the sacrifices made by die-hard sports fans in the form of time, money, and emotional energy may seem to outweigh the benefits.[13] Yet a closer look reveals that these investments yield social and psychological rewards far greater than they initially appear. Much like a high-stakes game, the payoff comes not only in fleeting moments of glory but also in a resounding sense of purpose. Sports fandom provides an avenue for managing life's uncertainties, offering clarity in a chaotic world. Fans simplify the complexity of existence by aligning themselves with teams and athletes, using their faith as a cognitive shortcut. This belief system offers meaning, stability, and a refuge from life's challenges. It could come in many forms, including the hope inspired by Morocco's football success or the camaraderie of Egyptian handball supporters. Sports offer an enduring beacon of optimism.

Fandom helps alleviate hardwired existential anxieties. The shared rituals and collective identities of fan communities help individuals feel less alone, providing an emotional safety net. The support system often extends beyond the realm of sports, fostering friendships and solidarity during life's hardships. Fandom further creates structure, offering a framework for social order and recognition. Hierarchies based on passion and commitment allow fans from all walks of life to gain respect and a sense of achievement within their communities. Meritocracy is especially evident in the dedication of fans who consistently attend local games or actively contribute to fan forums.[14]

Perhaps most significantly, sports fandom highlights the interplay between personal identity and group narratives.[15] As fans immerse themselves in their team's story, their own life narratives intertwine with that of the group and create a sense of common destiny. The dynamic is evident in the way supporters rally behind teams facing adversity, like when the Chicago Cubs broke their World Series curse or when South Africa's national cricket team strived for redemption on the global stage.

In essence, belief through sports fandom acts as a form of psychological armor. It shields fans from doubt, offers hope in the face of adversity, and unites individuals into cohesive communities. Like breathing, the act of believing in something greater than oneself is both unconscious and vital, shaping how fans navigate life's uncertainties. Ultimately, the rituals, narratives, and emotions tied to sports fandom create a microcosm of life itself. Whether through victory or defeat, joy or sorrow, the shared journey of fandom captures the essence of what it means to be a human seeking meaning in life: to belong, to hope, to believe, and to matter.

BOOK CHAPTER SUMMARY

In *The Psychology of Sports Fans*, I have reviewed the multifaceted psychological reasons behind the intense and often unwavering devotion of sports enthusiasts. Across its five chapters, the book explored how cognitive, emotional, and social processes shape the fan experience, illuminating why people are drawn to sports and what sustains their passion.

The journey began in Chapter 1: The Psychology of Sports Thinking, which examined the brain's natural inclination to adopt beliefs that foster social interaction and a sense of belonging. This foundational tendency drives fans to strongly identify with their teams, manifesting in behaviors such as wearing team apparel, attending games, and engaging in fan forums. Such activities reinforce group cohesion, creating a shared identity that intensifies the connection between fans and their teams.

Building on beliefs, Chapter 2: The Psychology of Sports Faith, explored the parallels between sports fandom and faith. The mind's predisposition to maintain loyalty and hope, even in the face of adversity, is central to the unwavering support fans exhibit for their teams. The chapter highlighted how fans rationalize failures, remain optimistic about future success, and often engage in superstitious rituals, reflecting steadfast and resilient faith in their teams.

Emotional intensity takes center stage in Chapter 3: The Psychology of Sports Emotions, which reveals how fans experience heightened emotions through their deep emotional investment in sports. The attribution of meaning and agency to game outcomes and team events magnifies feelings. Fans cheer, cry, and celebrate in response to victories or losses, forming emotional bonds with players and fellow fans that enrich their overall experience.

Going beyond 'normal' emotional experience, in Chapter 4: The Psychology of Sports Meaning, the narrative shifted to the profound sense of purpose and transcendence sports can offer. By providing opportunities for peak experiences and flow states, sports enable fans to feel moments of unity and significance analogous to spiritual practices. Rituals and traditions, often shared within fan communities, further enhance the feelings of meaning and belonging, elevating the sports experience far beyond mere entertainment.

Finally, this chapter, Chapter 5: The Psychology of Sports Fandom, synthesizes all the previous insights, emphasizing the role of overarching beliefs in simplifying decision-making and bolstering social cohesion. Fans adopt and fiercely defend sports beliefs, leading to an impenetrable shield of identity and community. Whether by attending games, participating in fan clubs, or standing firm against criticism, fans reinforce their commitment to their teams and the social bonds that come with it. Collectively, the five chapters I've presented help to explain the psychological forces at play in sports fandom, including how cognitive biases, emotional resonance, and the search for meaning converge to create a quintessentially human connection to the world of sports.

In the next part of the chapter, I present a framework for making sense of all the concepts I've detailed. I start by identifying some key elements of sport fan psychology and their positive and negative psychological implications. Then I assemble a general theory of sports fan psychology characterized by five hypotheses – propositions and principles – about how sports fan psychology works, as well as a summary of sport fandom's psychological benefits and costs. Later, I develop a more granular and specific theory and show how it explains the real-life behaviors of sports fans, leading to a 'typology', or a classification, of types of sports fans.

SPORTS FAN PSYCHOLOGY AND BELIEFS

My forthcoming theory centers around the concept of beliefs and how they interact with the human mind to create the phenomenon of fandom. It works as a reinforcing cycle via the following five steps.

1. Predisposition to Believe: Humans have evolved with an inherent tendency to believe, especially in things that offer personal and social benefits, such as belonging, identity, and meaning.
2. Exposure to Sports: When individuals are exposed to sports, their predisposition to believe interacts with culturally accessible content like teams, clubs, and players.
3. Formation of Sports Beliefs: Exposure leads to the formation of sports beliefs, often imbued with a sense of faith and conviction. These beliefs can range from factual to ideological and are often resistant to change despite contradictory evidence.
4. Cognitive Distortions: To protect faith-based sports beliefs, the mind employs various cognitive distortions and biases. The distortions further solidify beliefs and make them seem rational and unchallengeable to the fan.
5. Intensification of Fandom: Reinforced beliefs, in turn, intensify fandom, leading to greater emotional investment, ritualistic behaviors, and a heightened sense of belonging to the fan community.

PSYCHOLOGICAL BENEFITS AND COSTS OF SPORTS FANDOM

Sports fandom yields a suite of psychological benefits and costs, as summarized by the following five points on each.

<u>Benefits</u>

1. *Sense of Belonging and Community*: Sports fandom taps into a fundamental human need for connection and belonging. The shared experience of supporting a team, participating in rituals, and engaging in discussions with fellow fans fosters a strong sense of community and shared identity. This is particularly relevant in a world that can often feel isolating and fragmented.
2. *Enhanced Self-Esteem and Identity*: Identifying with a successful team can bolster self-esteem and provide a sense of pride and accomplishment. The association allows fans to vicariously experience the triumphs and achievements of their team, leading to an enhanced sense of self-worth.
3. *Meaning and Purpose*: Sports fandom can provide a sense of meaning and purpose in life, particularly for individuals who might otherwise struggle to find these elements. The dedication, passion, and shared goals associated with supporting a team can offer a framework for understanding and navigating the complexities of life.
4. *Emotional Regulation and Stress Relief*: Sports offer an outlet for emotional expression and release. The highs and lows of supporting a team can provide a cathartic experience, allowing fans to process and regulate their emotions. Additionally, the excitement and entertainment associated with sports can act as a distraction from daily stressors and anxieties.
5. *Optimism and Hope*: Sports fandom can promote optimism and hope, even in the face of adversity. The belief in the possibility of future success, the camaraderie of fellow fans, and the cyclical

nature of sports with its promise of new seasons and fresh starts can provide a psychological boost and a sense of anticipation.

Costs

1. *Cognitive Biases and Distorted Thinking*: Sports fandom can lead to cognitive biases and distortions in thinking. Fans can exhibit confirmation bias, selectively attending to information that supports their pre-existing beliefs about their team while dismissing or downplaying contradictory evidence. Biases can lead to unrealistic expectations, poor judgment, and difficulty accepting losses.
2. *Emotional Volatility and Stress*: While sports can offer a form of emotional release, they can also contribute to emotional instability and stress. The intense emotions associated with game outcomes, player performance, and team rivalries can lead to significant mood swings, anxiety, and even depression, particularly for those deeply invested in their team's success.
3. *Fanaticism and Irrational Behavior*: Extreme fandom can manifest in fanaticism and irrational behavior, which can involve obsessive following of the team, aggression toward rival fans, and a willingness to engage in risky or harmful actions in the name of team loyalty. In such cases, sports fandom can become detrimental to an individual's well-being and social relationships, and can sometimes lead to anti-social behavior.
4. *Diminished Critical Thinking and Objectivity*: Sports fandom can undermine critical thinking and objectivity. The strong emotional investment and the need to maintain a positive image of one's team can encourage a reluctance to acknowledge shortcomings or engage in balanced, reasoned analysis. The combination can have unwelcome implications for decision-making and interactions with those who hold different perspectives.
5. *Potential for Addiction and Time Consumption*: For some individuals, sports fandom can become all-consuming, leading to an unhealthy obsession with the team and possible neglect of other important

areas of life. The constant stream of games, news, and social media interactions can create a cycle of addiction and time consumption, impacting personal relationships, work, and overall well-being.

A GENERAL THEORY OF SPORT FAN PSYCHOLOGY

My general theory of sport fan psychology can be articulated through a series of six hypotheses, or premises, that culminate in an overarching theoretical proposition. Each hypothesis is accompanied by predictions that explain how sport fan psychology works in practice through fan behavior.

The first hypothesis proposes that sports hold immense significance for many individuals due to the human psyche's natural inclination toward strong beliefs and fanaticism. The inclination is founded in the brain's evolved tendency to embrace beliefs that aid in survival and social interaction. The hypothesis predicts that fans will exhibit behaviors that demonstrate strong loyalty and commitment to their teams, such as attending games regularly, wearing team merchandise, and participating in fan communities. These behaviors fulfill the need for social interaction and belonging.

The second hypothesis proposes that fans develop deeply ingrained belief systems around sports, which are resistant to change and operate like religious beliefs. Fan belief systems are reinforced by cognitive biases such as confirmation bias and optimism bias, and by the tendency to see patterns and agency in random events. Emotional experiences related to sports are strongly encoded in memory, making sports a significant part of a fan's identity. The hypothesis predicts that fans might interpret ambiguous events in a way that favors their team, such as blaming referees for losses or attributing wins to the team's inherent superiority, thereby reinforcing their belief system and strengthening their identity as fans.

The third hypothesis proposes that fans seek emotional coherence between their beliefs and experiences, leading to intense emotional reactions to sports events. Sports can induce peak experiences or flow states, characterized by deep immersion and emotional highs. Fans empathize with players and other fans, creating shared experiences and communities. The hypothesis predicts that fans will experience strong emotional reactions to game outcomes, such as euphoria after a win or despair after a loss. Emotional highs and lows will be shared within the fan community, enhancing the sense of belonging and mutual support.

The fourth hypothesis addresses the social dynamics of sports fandom, proposing that it fulfills the human need for belonging and identity. It often manifests in tribal behaviors and strong group identification. Fans engage in rituals and use symbols, such as team colors and chants, to express their allegiance and reinforce group cohesion. Social learning plays a crucial role, as fans learn behaviors and beliefs from other fans, often starting from a young age through family and community influence. The hypothesis predicts that fans will participate in pre-game and post-game rituals, such as tailgating, chanting, and wearing team colors. The behaviors reinforce group identity and cohesion, making fans feel part of a larger community.

The fifth hypothesis highlights the psychological benefits of sports fandom, including escapism, entertainment, and a sense of meaning and purpose. It proposes that being part of a fan community provides social support and a sense of belonging, which can fill existential voids. The hypothesis predicts that fans will use sports to escape from daily stresses and find joy and excitement. They will also derive a sense of purpose and identity from their association with their team, which can help mitigate feelings of loneliness, meaninglessness, or purposelessness.

The sixth hypothesis acknowledges the challenges and pathologies associated with extreme fandom. It proposes that fanaticism can lead to irrational beliefs and extreme behaviors, while the emotional highs and lows of sports can cause significant psychological stress, including anxiety and depression. Intense rivalries can also lead to conflict and aggression between fan groups. The hypothesis predicts that extreme fans may exhibit behaviors such as aggression toward rival fans, obsessive following of their team, and significant mood swings based on game outcomes. These behaviors can lead to personal and social conflicts, as well as mental health issues.

The six hypotheses lead to the overarching proposition that sport fan psychology is a complex interplay of cognitive biases, emotional engagement, and social forces. The dynamic interplay explains why sports hold such significance for many people. While fandom can provide numerous psychological benefits, it also has the potential to lead to extreme behaviors and emotional volatility. The general theory of sports fan psychology provides a framework for organizing the psychological structure that sports fans experience. Now, I will add a specific theory that I've termed the 'Cognitive-Emotional Resonance Theory (CERT)', to add more granularity by explaining the psychological mechanisms behind the hypotheses.

SPORT FAN PSYCHOLOGY COGNITIVE-EMOTIONAL RESONANCE THEORY (CERT)

Sport fandom is a multifaceted phenomenon based in cognitive, emotional, and social processes that shape human behavior. The Sport Fan Psychology Cognitive-Emotional Resonance Theory (CERT) exposes the mechanisms enabling tribalism and pattern recognition, which predispose individuals to see their team's journey as part of a meaningful narrative. Emotional anchors like coherence and flow states highlight the profound psychological impact of aligning fans' feelings with their team's performance. Social and cultural reinforcements, including rituals and shared symbols, foster group identity and solidarity, while cognitive biases shape fans' belief systems. CERT illuminates how sport fandom satisfies deep-seated human needs, often with both inspiring and troubling consequences. The key elements are summarized in five CERT dimensions followed by examples of how they explain different forms of fan behavior.

CERT DIMENSIONS

COGNITIVE FOUNDATIONS

- Innate Cognitive Structures: Brains are naturally predisposed to believe in certain concepts that aid survival and social cohesion. These include tribalism, identity, and belonging, which are all central to sport fandom.
- Pattern Recognition and Agency Detection: The mind is wired to detect patterns and assign agency, leading fans to see their team's successes and failures as part of a larger narrative or destiny.

EMOTIONAL ANCHORS

- Emotional Coherence: Fans seek emotional coherence, aligning their thoughts and feelings with their team's performance. This alignment provides psychological stability and reduces cognitive dissonance.
- Peak Experiences and Flow States: Intense engagement with sport can lead to peak experiences and flow states, where fans feel a deep connection to the game and their team, often described as transcendent or spiritual.

SOCIAL AND CULTURAL REINFORCEMENT

- Rituals and Symbols: Sport rituals (e.g., chants, wearing team colors) and symbols (e.g., logos, mascots) reinforce group identity and solidarity. These rituals are performed automatically, bypassing critical reflection and embedding deeply in the fan's psyche.
- Social Bonding: Shared experiences and collective rituals strengthen social bonds among fans, creating a sense of community and belonging.

COGNITIVE BIASES AND BELIEF SYSTEMS

- Confirmation Bias: Fans tend to seek out information that confirms their pre-existing beliefs about their team, leading to a biased interpretation of events.
- Counterintuitive Concepts: Sport beliefs often contain counter-intuitive elements (e.g., superstition, hope against odds) that make them more memorable and resilient.

PSYCHOLOGICAL BENEFITS

- Meaning and Purpose: Sport provides fans with a sense of meaning and purpose, helping them navigate life's uncertainties and challenges.
- Emotional Regulation: Engaging with sport helps fans regulate their emotions, providing an outlet for stress and a source of joy and excitement.

EXPLAINING SPORT FAN BEHAVIOR WITH CERT

LOYALTY AND COMMITMENT

- Deep Cognitive and Emotional Investment: Fans' loyalty to their team is driven by deep cognitive and emotional investments. The rituals, symbols, and shared experiences create a strong sense of identity and belonging.
- Resistance to Change: Due to cognitive biases like confirmation bias, fans are resistant to changing their allegiance, even in the face of poor team performance.

RITUALISTIC BEHAVIOR

- Automatic Performance of Rituals: Fans engage in rituals auto-matically, without questioning their utility. These rituals reinforce group identity and provide emotional comfort.

- Symbolic Actions: Actions like wearing team colors or singing the club anthem are symbolic, signaling commitment and belonging to the fan community.

EMOTIONAL REACTIONS

- Intense Emotional Responses: Fans experience intense emotional reactions to their team's performance, driven by the deep cognitive and emotional connections they have formed.
- Emotional Coherence: Fans align their emotions with their team's fortunes, experiencing joy in victory and despair in defeat.

SOCIAL DYNAMICS

- In-Group Solidarity: Fans exhibit strong in-group solidarity, supporting each other and reinforcing shared beliefs and values.
- Out-Group Hostility: Rivalries with other teams and their fans can lead to out-group hostility, further strengthening in-group bonds.

COGNITIVE AND EMOTIONAL BENEFITS

- Psychological Stability: The cognitive and emotional coherence provided by sport fandom helps fans maintain psychological stability.
- Stress Relief and Joy: Engaging with sport provides an outlet for stress and a source of joy, contributing to overall well-being.

EXPLAINING EXTREME FAN BEHAVIORS WITH CERT

COGNITIVE FACTORS

- Superordinate Beliefs: Fans' superordinate beliefs about their team can become so deeply ingrained that they override other rational considerations. This can lead to extreme behaviors as fans act in ways that they believe are necessary to support or defend their team.

- Confirmation Bias: Fans are prone to seeking out information that confirms their existing beliefs and ignoring contradictory evidence. This can lead to a distorted view of reality where any action taken in support of the team is justified, even if it involves violence or obsessive behavior.

EMOTIONAL FACTORS

- Emotional Coherence: Fans align their emotions with their team's performance, experiencing intense highs and lows. This emotional investment can lead to extreme reactions, such as violence after a loss or obsessive behavior to maintain a connection with the team.
- Peak Experiences: The intense engagement and peak experiences associated with sport fandom can create a powerful emotional bond that fans are unwilling to break, leading to obsessive behaviors to maintain that connection.

SOCIAL FACTORS

- In-Group Solidarity: Strong in-group solidarity among fans can lead to a 'mob mentality', where individuals feel justified in engaging in extreme behaviors because they are supported by the group. This can result in violence against rival fans or obsessive actions to prove loyalty.
- Rituals and Symbols: The rituals and symbols associated with sport fandom reinforce group identity and can escalate extreme behaviors. For example, fans might engage in violent rituals or obsessive collection of team memorabilia to demonstrate their commitment.

PSYCHOLOGICAL BENEFITS

- Meaning and Purpose: For some fans, their identity and sense of purpose are heavily tied to their team. This can lead to obsessive behaviors as they seek to maintain their connection to the team and the meaning it provides in their lives.
- Emotional Regulation: Engaging in extreme behaviors can be a way for fans to regulate their emotions, especially in response to the highs and lows of their team's performance. Violence or obsession can serve as outlets for the intense emotions they experience.

EXAMPLES OF EXTREME FAN BEHAVIORS EXPLAINED BY CERT

VIOLENCE

- Rivalry and Hostility: Fans may engage in violence against rival fans to defend their team's honor and assert dominance. This behavior is reinforced by in-group solidarity and the emotional highs and lows associated with the team's performance.
- Mob Mentality: During games or events, the collective energy and emotional investment of the crowd can lead to a mob mentality, where individuals feel empowered to act violently because they are supported by the group.

OBSESSION

- Collecting Memorabilia: Fans may obsessively collect team memorabilia to maintain a connection with their team and demonstrate their loyalty. This behavior is reinforced by the emotional significance of the items and the rituals associated with collecting.
- Stalking Players: In extreme cases, fans may become obsessed with individual players, engaging in stalking behaviors to feel closer to them. This can be driven by the intense emotional bond they feel and the desire to be part of the player's life.

Table 5.1 Psychological Typology of Sports Fan Types

High	*Analytical Observer*	*Social Connector*
	Maintains detailed statistics, writes analytical blogs, engages in discussions	Leads chants, organizes events, fosters inclusivity
	Creative Enthusiast	*Passionate Loyalist*
	Creates fan art, writes fan fiction, develops unique chants and rituals	Displays unwavering support, participates in all rituals, defends team passionately
Cognitive- Emotional Engagement	*Ritualistic Devotee*	*Impulsive Fanatic*
	Follows rituals meticulously, participates in choreographed displays	Engages in spontaneous actions, experiences thrill from impulsive behaviors
	Detached Spectator	*Emotional Reactor*
	Watches games for enjoyment and analysis, less involved in fan communities	Exhibits visible emotional reactions, seeks support during highs and lows
Low	Low **Social-Behavioral Engagement** High	

PSYCHOLOGICAL TYPOLOGY OF SPORT FAN TYPES

In this section I present a psychological typology (classification) of sport fan types. There are eight types of sport fans, each one represented by a quadrant created by a combination of high/low cognitive-emotional and social-behavioral engagement. In Table 5.1, the X-axis represents combined cognitive-emotional engagement, ranging from low to high, while the Y-axis represents social-behavioral engagement, also ranging from low to high. Table 5.2 summarizes the features of each type.

CONCLUSION: THE FINAL WHISTLE

In this book I have proposed that the intense and often irrational attachments fans develop toward their teams arise from a dynamic

Table 5.2 Descriptions of Sports Fan Types

Type	Cognitive Factors	Emotional Factors	Social Factors	Behavioral Factors
Social Connector	Engages deeply with social aspects of fandom, seeking out group activities and interactions.	Derives joy and fulfillment from social connections and group solidarity.	Highly active in fan communities, organizing and participating in group events and rituals.	Leads chants, organizes tailgate parties, fosters a welcoming atmosphere for other fans.
Analytical Observer	Focuses on detailed analysis and understanding of the game.	Experiences satisfaction from structured activities and in-depth analysis.	Provides valuable insights and resources to the fan community through blogs or forums.	Maintains detailed statistics, writes analytical blogs, engages in discussions about game strategies.
Creative Enthusiast	Seeks novel and creative ways to express fandom.	Experiences excitement and joy from creative expression and spontaneous actions.	Inspires other fans with unique and creative contributions, such as fan art or custom merchandise.	Creates fan art, writes fan fiction, develops unique chants and rituals.
Passionate Loyalist	Holds strong superordinate beliefs in team loyalty and identity.	Experiences intense emotional highs and lows based on the team's performance.	Deeply embedded in the fan community, often seen as a die-hard supporter.	Displays unwavering support, participates in all fan rituals, defends the team passionately.
Ritualistic Devotee	Adheres strictly to fan rituals and traditions.	Finds comfort and stability in repetitive and ritualistic behaviors.	Participates in and sometimes leads traditional fan rituals, reinforcing group identity.	Follows pre-game and post-game rituals meticulously, participates in choreographed displays.

Emotional Reactor	Prone to intense emotional reactions.	Experiences extreme emotional responses to the team's performance, both positive and negative.	Seeks support from the fan community during emotional highs and lows.	Exhibits visible emotional reactions, such as crying after a loss or ecstatic celebrations after a win.
Impulsive Fanatic	Prone to spontaneous and sometimes reckless behaviors.	Experiences thrill and excitement from impulsive actions related to fandom.	Often seen as a passionate and unpredictable member of the fan community.	Engages in spontaneous actions like rushing the field, making last-minute travel plans for away games.
Detached Spectator	Engages with the sport primarily for entertainment and intellectual stimulation.	Maintains a more detached and analytical perspective, with lower emotional investment.	Less involved in fan communities, prefers solitary or small group viewing.	Watches games for enjoyment and analysis but does not participate in fan rituals or community activities.

interplay of cognitive biases, emotional engagement, social dynamics, and behavioral responses. I've tried to explain the psychological mechanisms that fuel the fervor of sports fandom, and reveal how belief, emotion, and social connection intertwine to create this universal phenomenon.

My explanation for sport fan psychology highlights the **cognitive foundations** of fandom, housed in the brain's innate tendencies. Humans are naturally predisposed to form strong beliefs, particularly those that foster social cohesion and survival. This evolutionary trait makes sports a compelling vehicle for shared identity and belonging. Additionally, the brain's propensity for pattern recognition and agency detection drives fans to construct narratives around their teams' successes and failures, often interpreting random events as evidence of destiny or external influence. The tendencies solidify fans' deep emotional investment and reinforce the meaningful narratives they associate with sports.

Emotional anchors further deepen the attachments. Fans seek emotional coherence, aligning their feelings with their team's journey to minimize cognitive dissonance. For instance, rationalizing a loss by emphasizing effort over outcome helps fans maintain their emotional connection. Moreover, the intense immersion sports can evoke often leads to peak experiences and flow states. Such moments, characterized by a sense of transcendence and heightened focus, resonate deeply, creating emotional memories that bind fans to their teams. Such experiences are often described as spiritual, adding profound meaning to the act of fandom.

The **social and cultural reinforcement** of sports fandom strengthens its grip on individuals. Rituals, chants, and symbols like team colors and logos are integral in creating a shared identity among fans. Collective acts bypass critical reflection, embedding themselves in the fan's psyche and shaping their emotional responses. Beyond rituals, the communal nature of sports provides opportunities for social bonding through shared emotional highs and lows. Connections foster camaraderie and mitigate feelings of loneliness, enhancing psychological well-being and reinforcing a sense of belonging.

Sports fandom is also sustained by **cognitive biases and belief systems**. Confirmation bias plays a central role, as fans prioritize information that aligns with their existing beliefs about their teams while dismissing contradictions. A selective perspective protects fans' emotional investment and strengthens their loyalty. Fans are also drawn to counterintuitive beliefs, such as superstitions or improbable hopes, which, due to their unusual nature, are more memorable and resistant to change. Beliefs provide a sense of meaning and control, even in the face of unpredictability.

Ultimately, my explanation emphasizes the **psychological benefits** of sports fandom. By offering a framework for meaning and purpose, fandom allows individuals to align with a team's values and derive a sense of identity that transcends personal experience. Connection is especially significant during challenging times, serving as a source of hope and resilience. Additionally, sports fandom provides a controlled outlet for emotional expression, enabling fans to experience a spectrum of emotions like joy, disappointment, excitement, and catharsis that contribute to emotional regulation and overall well-being. Despite the often-irrational nature of behaviors, sport fandom fulfills fundamental psychological needs, offering connection, purpose, and emotional stability in an unpredictable world.

NOTES

1 Butler, M., Brar, G., Abed, R., & O'Connell, H. (2025). The people's game: Evolutionary perspectives on the behavioural neuroscience of football fandom. Frontiers in Psychology, 15, 1517295.

2 Archer, A., & Wojtowicz, J. (2023). Why It's OK to be a Sports Fan. Taylor & Francis.

3 Burton-Chellew, M. N., & West, S. A. (2012). Pseudocompetition among groups increases human cooperation in a public goods game. Animal Behaviour, 84(4), 947–952.

4 Yoshida, M., Gordon, B., James, J. D., & Heere, B. (2015). Sport fans and their behavior in fan communities. In K. Kanosue, K. Kogiso, D. Oshimi, & M. Harada (Eds.), Sports management and sports humanities (pp. 89–101). Springer.

5 Sierra, J. J., Taute, H. A., & Lee, B. K. (2022). Sport fans' defense of the tribal brand. In R. M. Crabtree & J. J. Zhang (Eds.), *Sport marketing in a global environment: Strategic perspectives* (pp. 142–160). Routledge.

6 Samra, B., & Wos, A. (2014). Consumer in sports: Fan typology analysis. *Journal of Intercultural Management*, 6(4), 263–288.

7 Jang, N., Chang, J., & Kim, Y. (2021). The effect of cognitive and affective trust on sport fan behavior after team's loss: A case of the US men's national soccer team viewership. *Korean Journal of Sport Science*, 32(2), 288–306.

8 Murrell, A. J., & Gaertner, S. L. (1992). Cohesion and sport team effectiveness: The benefit of a common group identity. *Journal of Sport and Social Issues*, 16(1), 1–14.

9 Berendt, J., & Uhrich, S. (2016). Enemies with benefits: The dual role of rivalry in shaping sports fans' identity. *European Sport Management Quarterly*, 16(5), 613–634.

10 Wann, D. L., & Grieve, F. G. (2008). The coping strategies of highly identified fans: The importance of team success on tendencies to utilize proactive pessimism. In L. W. Hugenberg, P. Haridakis, & A. Earnheardt (Eds.), *Media and mediated sports fandom* (pp. 29–44). McFarland.

11 Newson, M., Buhrmester, M., & Whitehouse, H. (2023). United in defeat: Shared suffering and group bonding among football fans. *Managing Sport and Leisure*, 28(2), 164–181.

12 Delia, E. B., James, J. D., & Wann, D. L. (2021). Does being a sport fan provide meaning in life? *Journal of Sport Management*, 36(1), 45–55.

13 Norris, J. I., Wann, D. L., & Zapalac, R. K. (2015). Sport fan maximizing: Following the best team or being the best fan? *Journal of Consumer Marketing*, 32(3), 157–166.

14 Reysen, S., & Branscombe, N. R. (2010). Fanship and fandom: Comparisons between sport and non-sport fans. *Journal of Sport Behavior*, 33(2), 176–193.

15 Cottingham, M. D. (2012). Interaction ritual theory and sports fans: Emotion, symbols, and solidarity. *Sociology of Sport Journal*, 29(2), 168–185.

FURTHER RESOURCES

RECOMMENDED READING

Abeza, G., O'Reilly, N., Sanderson, J., & Frederick, E. (2021). *Social media in sport: Theory and practice*. World Scientific.

Chadwick, S., Chanavat, N., & Desbordes, M. (2016). *Routledge handbook of sports marketing*. Routledge.

Dees, W., Walsh, P., McEvoy, C. D., McKelvey, S., Mullin, B. J., Hardy, S., & Sutton, W. A. (2021). *Sport marketing*. Human Kinetics.

Fullerton, S. (2021). *Sports marketing*. SAGE Publications.

Funk, D. C., Alexandris, K., & McDonald, H. (2022). *Sport consumer behaviour*. Routledge.

Hoye, R., Smith, A., Stewart, B., & Nicholson, M. (2015). *Sport management: Principles and applications* (4th ed.). Elsevier.

Hums, M. A., Kluch, Y., Schmidt, S. H., & MacLean, J. C. (2023). *Governance and policy in sport organizations*. Taylor & Francis.

Karg, A., Shilbury, D., Westerbeek, H., Funk, D. C., & Naraine, M. L. (2022). *Strategic sport marketing* (5th ed.). Routledge.

Kingsnorth, S. (2022). *Digital marketing strategy: An integrated approach to online marketing*. Kogan Page.

Lough, N., & Geurin, A. N. (Eds.). (2019). *Routledge handbook of the business of women's sport*. Routledge.

Pedersen, P. M., Laucella, P. C., Kian, E. M., & Geurin, A. N. (2021). *Strategic sport communication.* Human Kinetics.

Ratten, V. (2019). *Sports technology and innovation.* Springer Books.

Sarver Coombs, D., & Osborne, A. C. (2022). *Routledge handbook of sports fans and fandom.* Routledge.

Schmidt, S. L. (Ed.). (2020). *21st century sports: How technologies will change sports in the digital age.* Springer Nature.

Seymour, A., & Blakey, P. (2021). *Digital sport marketing: Concepts, cases, and conversations.* Routledge.

Smith, A. C. T. (2023). *Football on the brain: Why minds love sport.* Margin Press.

Smith, A. C. T., Stavros, C., & Westberg, K. (2017). *Brand fans: Lessons from the world's greatest sporting brands.* Palgrave Macmillan.

Stavros, C., & Smith, A. C. T. (2021). *Sport branding insights.* Routledge.

Stoldt, G. C., Dittmore, S. W., Ross, M., & Branvold, S. E. (2020). *Sport public relations.* Human Kinetics.

Wann, D. L., & James, J. D. (2019). *Sport fans: The psychology and social impact of fandom.* Routledge.

Woods, R., & Butler, B. N. (2020). *Social issues in sport.* Human Kinetics.

ONLINE RESOURCES

American Psychological Association (APA) Podcast: Daniel Wann. 2025. www.apa.org/news/podcasts/speaking-of-psychology/sports-fans

North American Society for Sport Management. 2025. https://nassm.org

The Psychology Behind Sports Fans – Trevor Hecht. 2025. www.youtube.com/watch?v=q2bhskk17ng

Sport Management Association of Australia and New Zealand. 2025. www.smaanz.org

The Strange Psychology of Superfans – PBS. 2025. www.youtube.com/watch?v=RYySvUwbmGg

Why are football fans so obsessed? – Becky Spelman. 2025.www.youtube.com/watch?v=ZfHDpIIrJl4

Why Do People Obsess Over Sports? – Eric Simons. 2025. www.youtube.com/watch?v=ImW73w64MlM

BIBLIOGRAPHY

Aglioti, S. M., Cesari, P., Romani, M., & Urgesi, C. (2008). Action anticipation and motor resonance in elite basketball players. *Nature Neuroscience*, 11, 1109–1116.

Alcorta, C. S., & Sosis, R. (2005). Ritual, emotion, and sacred symbols. *Human Nature*, 16(4), 323–335.

Ambady, N., & Bharucha, J. (2009). Culture and the brain. *Current Directions in Psychological Science*, 18(6), 342–345.

Ambler, T., Braeutigam, S., Stins, J., Rose, S., & Swithenby, S. (2004). Salience and choice: Neural correlates of shopping decisions. *Psychology & Marketing*, 21(4), 247–261.

Andersen, S. C., & Hjortskov, M. (2015). Cognitive biases in performance evaluations. *Journal of Public Administration Research and Theory*, 26(4), 647–662.

Aoki, C., Romeo, R. D., & Smith, S. S. (2017). Adolescence as a critical period for developmental plasticity. *Brain Research*, 1654, 85–86.

Austin, J. (1998). *Zen and the brain*. MIT Press.

Barnes, J. L. (2015). Fanfiction as imaginary play: What fan-written stories can tell us about the cognitive science of fiction. *Poetics*, 48, 69–82.

Bell, V., & Halligan, P. W. (2013). The neural basis of abnormal personal belief. In F. Krueger & J. Grafman (Eds.), *The neural basis of human belief systems* (pp. 191–224). Hove Psychology Press.

Belle, N., Cantarelli, P., & Belardinelli, P. (2017). Cognitive biases in performance appraisal: Experimental evidence on anchoring and halo effects with public sector managers and employees. *Review of Public Personnel Administration*, 37(3), 275–294.

Bernardin, H. J., Thomason, S., Buckley, M. R., & Kane, J. S. (2016). Rater rating-level bias and accuracy in performance appraisals: The impact of rater personality, performance management competence, and rater accountability. *Human Resource Management*, 55(2), 321–340.

Bol, J. C. (2011). The determinants and performance effects of managers' performance evaluation biases. *Accounting Review*, 86(5), 1549–1575.

Boyd, R. T., & Richerson, P. J. (2009). Culture and the evolution of human cooperation. *Philosophical Transactions of the Royal Society B: Biological Sciences*, 364(1533), 3281–3288.

Bracha, A., & Brown, D. J. (2012). Affective decision making: A theory of optimism bias. *Games and Economic Behavior*, 75, 67–80.

Breuer, K., Nieken, P., & Sliwka, D. (2013). Social ties and subjective performance evaluations: An empirical investigation. *Review of Managerial Science*, 7(2), 141–157.

Browne, M., Thomson, P., Rockloff, M. J., & Pennycook, G. (2015). Going against the herd: Psychological and cultural factors underlying the 'vaccination confidence gap'. *PLoS One*, 10(9), e0132562.

Buhrmester, M., Fraser, W. T., Lanman, J. A., Whitehouse, H., & Swann, W. B. (2015). When terror hits home: Identity fused Americans who saw Boston bombing victims as 'family' provided aid. *Self and Identity*, 14(3), 253–270.

Burton-Chellew, M. N., & West, S. A. (2012). Pseudocompetition among groups increases human cooperation in a public goods game. *Animal Behaviour*, 84(4), 947–952.

Calvo-Merino, B., Glaser, D. E., Grèzes, J., Passingham, R. E., & Haggard, P. (2005). Action observations and acquired motor skills: An fMRI study with expert dancers. *Cerebral Cortex*, 15, 1243–1249.

Cavojov, A. V., Srol, J., & Jurkovi, C. M. (2020). Why should we try to think like scientists? Scientific reasoning and susceptibility to epistemically suspect beliefs and cognitive biases. *Applied Cognitive Psychology*, 34(1), 85–95.

Choi, J.-K., & Bowles, S. (2007). The coevolution of parochial altruism and war. *Science*, 318(5850), 636–640.

Cohen, E. L., Atwell Seate, A., Anderson, S. M., & Tindage, M. F. (2017). Sport fans and Sci-Fi fanatics: The social stigma of popular media fandom. *Psychology of Popular Media Culture*, 6(3), 193–207.

Connors, M. H., & Halligan, P. W. (2015). A cognitive account of belief: A tentative road map. *Frontiers in Psychology*, 5, 1–14.

Csikszentmihalyi, M. (1990). *Flow: The psychology of optimal experience*. Harper & Row.

D'Acremont, M., Schultz, W., & Bossaerts, P. (2013). The human brain encodes event frequencies while forming subjective beliefs. *Journal of Neuroscience*, 33(26), 10887–10897.

Damasio, A. R. (2000). Thinking about belief. In D. L. Schacter & E. Scarry (Eds.), *Memory, brain and belief* (pp. 325–334). Harvard University Press.

Decety, J., Pape, R., & Workman, C. I. (2018). A multilevel social neuroscience perspective on radicalization and terrorism. *Social Neuroscience*, 13(5), 511–529.

Delfgaauw, J., & Souverijn, M. (2016). Biased supervision. *Journal of Economic Behavior and Organization*, 130, 107–125.

Diesendruck, G. (2013). Essentialism: The development of a simple, but potentially dangerous, idea. In M. Banaji & S. Gelman (Eds.), *Navigating the social world: What infants, children, and other species can teach us* (pp. 263–268). Oxford University Press.

Duarte, I. C., Afonso, S., Jorge, H., Cayolla, R., Ferreira, C., & Castelo-Branco, M. (2017). Tribal love: The neural correlates of passionate engagement in football fans. *Social Cognitive and Affective Neuroscience*, 12(5), 718–728.

Dwyer, B., Slavich, M. A., & Gellock, J. L. (2018). A fan's search for meaning: Testing the dimensionality of sport fan superstition. *Sport Management Review*, 21(5), 533–548.

Erikstad, M. K., & Johansen, B. T. (2020). Referee bias in professional football: Favoritism toward successful teams in potential penalty situations. *Frontiers in Sports and Active Living*, 2, 19.

Falk, E. B., & Lieberman, M. D. (2012). The neural bases of attitudes evaluations and behavior change. In F. Krueger & J. Grafman (Eds.), *The neural basis of human belief systems* (pp. 71–94). Taylor & Francis Psychology Press.

Ferris, D. L., Reb, J., Lian, H., Sim, S., & Ang, D. (2018). What goes up must... keep going up? Cultural differences in cognitive styles influence evaluations of dynamic performance. *Journal of Applied Psychology*, 103(3), 347–358.

Findlay, L. C., & Ste-Marie, D. M. (2004). A reputation bias in figure skating judging. *Journal of Sport and Exercise Psychology*, 26(1), 154–166.

Freeman, D., Dunn, G., Garety, P. A., Bebbington, P., Slater, M., Kuipers, E., Fowler, D., Green, C., Jordan, J., & Ray, K. (2005). The psychology of persecutory ideation I: A questionnaire survey. *Journal of Nervous and Mental Disease*, 193(5), 302–308.

Friston, K. (2010). The free-energy principle: A unified brain theory? *Nature Reviews Neuroscience*, 11, 127–138.

Galbraith, N., & Manktlow, K. (2014). A psychological model of delusional belief: Integrating reasoning biases with perceptual, self-concept and emotional factors. In N. Galbraith (Ed.), *Aberrant beliefs and reasoning* (pp. 19–45). Psychology Press.

Gilovich, T., Vallone, R., & Tversky, A. (1985). The hot hand in basketball: On the misperception of random sequences. *Cognitive Psychology*, 17(3), 295–314.

Halligan, P. (2007). Belief and illness. *Psychologist*, 20(6), 358–361.

Hamstra, M. R. (2014). 'Big' men: Male leaders' height positively relates to followers' perception of charisma. *Personality and Individual Differences*, 56, 190–192.

Han, S., Northoff, G., Vogeley, K., Wexler, B. E., Kitayama, S., & Varnum, M. E. (2013). A cultural neuroscience approach to the biosocial nature of the human brain. *Annual Review of Psychology*, 64, 335–359.

Hare, B. (2017). Survival of the friendliest: Homo sapiens evolved via selection for prosociality. *Annual Review of Psychology*, 68(1), 155–186.

Haselton, M. G., & Nettle, D. (2006) The paranoid optimist: An integrative evolutionary model of cognitive biases. *Personality and Social Psychology Review*, 10(1), 47–66.

Hogg, M. A., Kruglanski, A., & van den Bos, K. (2013). Uncertainty and the roots of extremism. *Journal of Social Issues*, 69(3), 407–418.

Horgan, J. (2014). *The psychology of terrorism* (2nd ed.). Routledge.

Howlett, J. R., & Paulus, M. P. (2015). The neural basis of testable and non-testable beliefs. *PloS One*, 10(5), 1–17.

Inzlicht, M., McGregor, I., Hirsh, J. B., & Nash, K. (2009). Neural markers of religious conviction. *Psychological Science*, 20(3), 385–392.

Kahneman, D. (2011). *Thinking, fast and slow*. Macmillan.

Kashima, Y., McKintyre, A., & Clifford, P. (1998). The category of the mind: Folk psychology of belief, desire, and intention. *Asian Journal of Social Psychology*, 1(3), 289–313.

Kitayama, S., & Uskul, A. K. (2011). Culture, mind, and the brain: Current evidence and future directions. *Annual Review of Psychology*, 62, 419–449.

Knowles, R., McCarthy-Jones, S., & Rowse, G. (2011). Grandiose delusions: A review and theoretical integration of cognitive and affective perspectives. *Clinical Psychology Review*, 31(4), 684–696.

Kovács, Á. M., Kühn, S., Gergely, G., Csibra, G., & Brass, M. (2014). Are all beliefs equal? Implicit belief attributions recruiting core brain regions of theory of mind. *PloS One, 9*(9), e106558.

Kruger, D. J., Falbo, M., Blanchard, S., Cole, E., Gazoul, C., Nader, N., & Murphy, S. (2018). University sports rivalries provide insights on coalitional psychology. *Human Nature, 29*(3), 337–352.

Kruger, J., & Dunning, D. (1999). Unskilled and unaware of it: How difficulties in recognizing one's own incompetence lead to inflated self-assessments. *Journal of Personal and Social Psychology, 77*, 1121–1134.

Krueger, F., & Grafman, J. (2012). I believe to my soul. In F. Krueger & J. Grafman (Eds.), *The neural basis of human belief systems* (pp. 225–236). Taylor & Francis.

Kuhnen, C. M., & Knutson, B. (2011). The influence of affect on beliefs, preferences, and financial decisions. *Journal of Financial and Quantitative Analysis, 46*(03), 605–626.

Kunda, Z. (1990). The case for motivated reasoning. *Psychological Bulletin, 108*(3), 480.

Kurzban, R., Burton-Chellew, M. N., & West, S. A. (2015). The evolution of altruism in humans. *Annual Review of Psychology, 66*(1), 575–599.

Laird, J. E., Lebiere, C., & Rosenbloom, P. S. (2017). A standard model of the mind: Toward a common computational framework across artificial intelligence, cognitive science, neuroscience, and robotics. *AI Magazine, 38*(4), 13–26.

Lewandowsky, S., Oberauer, K., & Gignac, G. (2013). NASA faked the moon landing – Therefore (climate) science is a hoax: An anatomy of the motivated rejection of science. *Psychological Science, 24*, 622–633.

Lindeman, M., & Lipsanen, J. (2016). Diverse cognitive profiles of religious believers and nonbelievers. *International Journal for the Psychology of Religion, 26*(3), 185–192.

Lovallo, D., & Kahneman, D. (2003). Delusions of success. *Harvard Business Review, 81*, 56–63.

Mandelbaum, E. (2019). Troubles with Bayesianism: An introduction to the psychological immune system. *Mind & Language, 34*(2), 141–157.

Mandelbaum, E., & Quilty-Dunn, J. (2015). Believing without reason or: Why liberals shouldn't watch Fox News. *The Harvard Review of Philosophy, 22*, 42–52.

Mar, R. A. (2011). The neural bases of social cognition and story comprehension. *Annual Review of Psychology, 62*, 103–134.

Marsh, E. J., & Stanley, M. L. (2020). False beliefs: Byproducts of an adaptive knowledge base? In R. Greifeneder, M. Jaffe, E. Newman & N. Schwarz (Eds.),

The psychology of fake news: Accepting, sharing, and correcting misinformation (pp. 131–146). Routledge.

McKay, R. T., & Dennett, D. C. (2009). The evolution of misbelief. Behavioral and Brain Sciences, 32(6), 493–495.

Mercier, H. (2016). Confirmation bias – Myside bias. In R. Pohl (Ed.), Cognitive illusions: Intriguing phenomena in judgement (pp. 109–124). Psychology Press.

Merkel, S., Chan, H. F., Schmidt, S. L., & Torgler, B. (2020). Optimism and positivity biases in performance appraisal ratings: Empirical evidence from professional soccer. Applied Psychology, 1100–1127.

Metz, S. E., Weisberg, D. S., & Weisberg, M. (2018). Non-scientific criteria for belief sustain counter-scientific beliefs. Cognitive Science, 42(5), 1477–1503.

Milfont, T. L., Milojev, P., Greaves, L. M., & Sibley, C. G. (2015). Socio-structural and psychological foundations of climate change beliefs. New Zealand Journal of Psychology, 44(1), 18–30.

Molden, D. C., & Higgins, E. T. (2012). Motivated thinking. In K. J. Holyoak & R. G. Morrison (Eds.), The Oxford handbook of thinking and reasoning (pp. 390–409). Oxford University Press.

Montibeller, G., & Von Winterfeldt, D. (2015). Cognitive and motivational biases in decision and risk analysis. Risk Analysis, 35(7), 1230–1251.

Morgulev, E., Azar, O. H., Lidor, R., Sabag, E., & Bar-Eli, M. (2018). Searching for judgment biases among elite basketball referees. Frontiers in Psychology, 9, 2637.

Morris, D. (1981). The soccer tribe. Jonathan Cape.

Morrison, A. P., Wells, A., & Nothard, S. (2000). Cognitive factors in predisposition to auditory and visual hallucinations. British Journal of Clinical Psychology, 39(1), 67–78.

Mukamel, R., Ekstrom, A. D., Kaplan, J., Iacoboni, M., & Fried, I. (2010). Single-neuron responses in humans during execution and observation of actions. Current Biology, 20, 750–756.

Newberg, A., & Lee, B. (2005). The neuroscientific study of religious and spiritual phenomena: Or why God doesn't use biostatistics. Zygon, 40(2), 469–490.

Newberg, A. B., D'Aquili, E., & Rause, V. (2001). Why God won't go away: Brain science and the biology of belief. Ballantine.

Newson, M., Bortolini, T., Buhrmester, M., da Silva, S., Acquino, J., & Whitehouse, H. (2018). Brazil's football warriors: Social bonding and inter-group violence. Evolution and Human Behavior, 39(6), 675–683.

Newson, M., Buhrmester, M., & Whitehouse, H. (2016). Explaining lifelong loyalty: The role of identity fusion and self-shaping group events. *PLoS One*, 11(8), e0160427.

Newson, M., Shiramizu, V., Buhrmester, M., Hattori, W., Jong, J., Yamamoto, E., & Whitehouse, H. (2020). Devoted fans release more cortisol when watching live soccer matches. *Stress and Health*, 36(2), 220–227.

Ng, K. Y., Koh, C., Ang, S., Kennedy, J. C., & Chan, K. Y. (2011). Rating leniency and halo in multisource feedback ratings: Testing cultural assumptions of power distance and individualism-collectivism. *Journal of Applied Psychology*, 96, 1033–1044.

Norman, G. R., Monteiro, S. D., Sherbino, J., Ilgen, J. S., Schmidt, H. G., & Mamede, S. (2017). The causes of errors in clinical reasoning: Cognitive biases, knowledge deficits, and dual process thinking. *Academic Medicine*, 92(1), 23–30.

Oatley, K. (2012). The cognitive science of fiction. *Wiley Interdisciplinary Reviews: Cognitive Science*, 3(4), 425–430.

Oatley, K. (1999). Why fiction may be twice as true as fact: Fiction as cognitive and emotional simulation. *Review of General Psychology*, 3(2), 101–117.

Oberai, H., & Anand, I. M. (2018). Unconscious bias: Thinking without thinking. *Human Resource Management International Digest*, 26(6), 14–17.

Palmer, C. L., & Peterson, R. D. (2016). Halo effects and the attractiveness premium in perceptions of political expertise. *American Politics Research*, 44(2), 353–382.

Park, D. C., & Huang, C-M. (2010). Culture wires the brain: A cognitive neuroscience perspective. *Perspectives on Psychological Science*, 5, 391–400.

Pemberton, A., & Aarten, P. G. M. (2017). Narrative in the study of victimological processes in terrorism and political violence: An initial exploration. *Studies in Conflict & Terrorism*, 41(7), 541–556.

Pennycook, G., Cheyne, J. A., Barr, N., Koehler, D. J., & Fugelsang, J. A. (2015). On the reception and detection of pseudo-profound bullshit. *Judgment and Decision Making*, 10(6), 549–563.

Pennycook, G., & Rand, D. G. (2021). The psychology of fake news. *Trends in Cognitive Sciences*, 25(5), 388–402.

Persinger, M. A. (2001). The neuropsychiatry of paranormal experiences. *Journal of Neuropsychiatry and Clinical Neuroscience*, 13(4), 515–524.

Pohl, R. F. (2017). Introduction: Cognitive illusions. In R. Pohl (Ed.), *Cognitive illusions: Intriguing phenomena in judgement* (pp. 3–21). Psychology Press.

Porot, N., & Mandelbaum, E. (2021). The science of belief: A progress report. *Wiley Interdisciplinary Reviews: Cognitive Science*, 12(2), e1539.

Rahman, T., Resnick, P. J., & Harry, B. (2016). Anders Breivik: Extreme beliefs mistaken for psychosis. *Journal of the American Academy of Psychiatry and the Law Online*, 44(1), 28–35.

Raiola, G., Tafuri, D., & Gomez Paloma, F. (2014). Physical activity and sport skills and its relation to mind theory on motor control. *Sport Science*, 7(1), 52–56.

Ramachandran, V. S., & Blakeslee, S. (1998). *Phantoms in the brain: Probing the mysteries of the mind*. Quill.

Rizeq, J., Flora, D. B., & Toplak, M. E. (2021). An examination of the underlying dimensional structure of three domains of contaminated mindware: Paranormal beliefs, conspiracy beliefs, and anti-science attitudes. *Thinking and Reasoning*, 27(2), 187–211.

Roets, A. (2017). 'Fake news': Incorrect, but hard to correct. The role of cognitive ability on the impact of false information on social impressions. *Intelligence*, 65, 107–110.

Rogers, L. J., & Kaplan, G. T. (2002). *Songs, roars, and rituals: Communication in birds, mammals, and other animals*. Harvard University Press.

Saucier, G. (2000). Isms and the structure of social attitudes. *Journal of Personality and Social Psychology*, 78(2), 366–385.

Saucier, G. (2013). Isms dimensions: Toward a more comprehensive and integrative model of belief-system components. *Journal of Personality and Social Psychology*, 104(5), 921–939.

Saver, J. L., & Rabin, J. (1997). The neural substrates of religious experience. *Journal of Neuropsychiatry Clinical Neuroscience*, 9(3), 498–510.

Schmack, K., de Castro, A. G. C., Rothkirch, M., Sekutowicz, M., Rössler, H., Haynes, J. D., & Sterzer, P. (2013). Delusions and the role of beliefs in perceptual inference. *Journal of Neuroscience*, 33(34), 13701–13712.

Sharot, T. (2011). The optimism bias. *Current Biology*, 21, R941–R945.